A WALK ON THE
WILD SIDE
WHEELCHAIR CRUISING IN THE PHILIPPINES AND JAPAN

MIKE FOX

Gotham Books

30 N Gould St.
Ste. 20820, Sheridan, WY 82801
https://gothambooksinc.com/

Phone: 1 (307) 464-7800

© 2025 *Mike Fox*. All rights reserved.

No part of this book may be reproduced, stored in a retrieval system, or transmitted by any means without the written permission of the author.

Published by Gotham Books (February 5, 2025)

 ISBN: 979-8-3483-0038-8 (P)
 ISBN: 979-8-3483-0039-5 (E)

Because of the dynamic nature of the Internet, any web addresses or links contained in this book may have changed since publication and may no longer be valid.

The views expressed in this work are solely those of the author and do not necessarily reflect the views of the publisher, and the publisher hereby disclaims any responsibility for them.

Contents

February - March 2023: Background 1

Thursday 16 February: A Green and Precious Land 3

Friday 17 February: Touching Down in Singapore 7

Saturday 18 February: Panicking in Singapore 8

Sunday 19 February: Getting to know Cebu 15

Monday 20 February: Historic Cebu 18

Tuesday 21 February: Projects and Plans 22

Wednesday 22 February: Of Mice and Men 25

Thursday 23 February: The Wedding 27

Friday 24 February: Plantation Bay 30

Saturday 25 February: The Swab Test 33

Sunday 26 February: Remembering Lapu Lapu 35

Monday 27 February: Calamity Strikes 38

Tuesday 28 February: A long day travelling to Tokyo 49

Wednesday 1 March: The Hama Rikyu Garden 51

Thursday 2 March: A Loyal Dog, Meeting up with Tomoru, A Palace and a Tower 53

Friday 3 March: Discovering the Wild Country of Nikko 58

Saturday 4 March: Trainspotting in Japan: Locomotive C11 123 and the Edo Wonder Train 63

Sunday 5 March: The Fellowship of St Alban's 67

Monday 6 March: The Limited Express to Matsumoto 82

Tuesday 7 March: Matsumoto Castle 86

Wednesday 8 March: The Trek to Kanazawa 90

Thursday 9 March: The Gardens of Kanazawa 93

Friday 10 March: Taking the Shinkansen to Hiroshima and meeting up with Fujio and his family 97

Saturday 11 March: The Peace Museum and an Unusual Bridge 101

Sunday 12 March: The Torii Gate at Miyajima 106

Monday 13 March: Travelling to Kyoto 109

Tuesday 14 March: Meeting Kyoko in Kyoto 112

Wednesday 15 March: The Super Express to Tokyo 120

Thursday 16 March: Sayonara Japan 125

Other Books by Mike Fox:

- Travelling by Road, Rail, Sea, Air (and Wheelchair) in North America

- Vamos a Brasil! Recollections of a Volunteer attempting to teach English in Brazil

- The Pivo Tour of Slovakia: Memoirs of an Anglo-Slovak student exchange – The observations of an Outsider

- The Italian Therapy Job: A Travel Diary

- The Wheelchair goes East – Hong Kong, Macau and Mainland China

- Brooklyn to Buenos Aires: Travelling down the Spine of the Americas

February - March 2023

Background

I blame our elder son, Nathan, for this adventure. He informed us around Christmas time that he was planning to marry his long-term girlfriend, Melodie, on her native island of Cebu in the Philippines, in February. There was no way Sylvia and I were going to miss this big occasion, which also led to our meeting Melodie's mom, Leticia, her daughter, KC, and other members of her family in addition to a prodigious number of dogs. Nathan then suggested that whilst we were in this part of the world, we ought to consider visiting Japan (as you do). Well, who could resist such a suggestion? He knew he was pushing at an open door. So, we just had to include Japan in our travels.

Around two decades ago, we were privileged to have the opportunity of sharing our home, as host parents, with several Japanese students, mostly teachers of English, who were studying the teaching of English at the local South Devon College. As soon as we had decided to add Japan on to our proposed travels, we set about trying to make contact with them and seeing whether we could meet up and maybe take them out for a meal and/or spend some time with them. In the end, we successfully linked up with three of our former students, Tomoru, Fujio and Kyoko, and our time in Japan was structured around meeting up with these three amazing people, all of whom gave up valuable time to significantly enhance the value of our trip to Japan.

This travelogue also focuses on the issues faced by my disabled wife, Sylvia, who needs to travel in a wheelchair nearly all of the time and who also has Parkinson's disease. There were several challenges along the way, all of which Sylvia rose to positively, and at times our journey became a real adventure, very occasionally descending into the sphere of chaos. But good people were on hand to assist and encourage us at every step of our journey. And what a journey it turned out to be!

Thursday 16 February

A Green and Precious Land

This turns out to be an even more chaotic morning than is usually the case when we set off on our travels. The main complication we face is the need to complete entry forms for Singapore (related to Covid), which are required to be signed within a matter of hours prior to take off for the city state, in addition to organising last minute medication for Sylvia, trying to sort out computer passwords, reacting to the possibility of rats in our garage (the sighting of one on the patio yesterday is a bit of a shock), and ensuring our packed cases are within the official weight limit, to avoid fines by the airlines.

Our good friend and next door neighbour, Kerry, volunteers to drive us to Newton Abbot Railway Station in her people mover, to catch our train to London. She says she has a lazy day ahead of her, and as soon as she has dropped us at the station, she aims to take a leisurely walk with her seven-year-old son, Joules, around a nearby lake in a country park and enjoy a picnic. I'm tempted to drop our travel plans and join her!

The over-enthusiastic station staff at Newton Abbot Station don't allow us to do anything by way of hauling our baggage. This is very kind of them, but it means that the real tests are yet to come in the adventure which is about to unfold before us.

The disabled seating is located within the first class zone of our train to London, which means that, despite buying standard class tickets, we also gain access to free coffee, water and snacks. So, it's not all bad news travelling by train with a wheelchair, or accompanying Sylvia as an (almost) able-bodied specimen, just relying on a single crutch most of the time, as I continue to recover from my hip surgery.

Our friendly Romanian hostess on the train points to my Japanese phrase book and remarks that she's impressed I am trying to learn the language. But the stark truth is that most words and phrases are going in one ear and out the other! I am working especially hard on mastering the Japanese phrase: "e . go ga ha . na . se . mas ka". (Do you speak English?)

Much of the fairly flat Somerset landscape is flooded before the train passes through the scenically delightful county of Wiltshire; the landscape is a pattern of green velvet, interlaced by a couple of canals, with farmsteads nestling in the re-entrants of shallow valleys. It radiates an ambience of peace and wellbeing, along a route I never tire of looking at from the train, having used it a lot for work in a previous life.

The junction of Reading is a good example of extensive investment in rail reconstruction in the UK, and the entire track layout has in recent years been expanded and electrified. Relatively new tracks in and around the station link the south coast, especially the port of Southampton, with the West Midlands, which is part of an ambitious electrification scheme. I think the station these days handles more trains than London Paddington. After passing high density, high rise office developments around the centre of Reading, we cross the River Thames and, very quickly, we are speeding through the Metropolitan Green Belt, which has retained its pleasant rural, green and open character in the face of considerable development pressures that this part of the UK has experienced for several decades.

Grey rain clouds gather ominously over the West London suburbs; Sylvia says she is impressed by the dramatic cloud formations. There is still quite a lot of evidence of cranes and construction sites, despite UK PLC nearly hitting recession last month. In particular, the area in and around Old Oak Common appears to be a hive of economic activity. I am amused by the huge display of graffiti at the Old Oak Common rail depot, proclaiming the slogan: "Eat Da Rich".

The disability staff are quickly on our case at Paddington, assisting us with our transfer to the Heathrow Express, but they must firstly wait patiently while Sylvia uses the station's facilities. Our son David rings to update me on various football matters; he is my trusted source of information on this important area of knowledge.

It's a relatively short and easy route after alighting from the Heathrow Express, via a lift, to the cavernous departure lounge in Terminal 5 at London's Heathrow Airport. After checking in, we wait around for a travel company courier to hand over to us our Japanese Rail (JR) passes and additional hotel information. Eventually, an hour after our appointed meeting time, our courier shows up, blaming heavy traffic congestion for his late arrival. He is all smiles and says he will see us later. Maybe, who knows?

The access staff persuade me to travel from the lounge to a far-flung gate, where our flight to Singapore is due to depart at 9:35pm. For some reason, Sylvia gets wheeled down to the departure gate well before me; I am also in a wheelchair at this point, and my pusher has to ring through to tell the cabin crew that we are on our way. I have visions of Sylvia and I ending up on separate planes!

Our plane, a Boeing 777, with both of us now aboard together, eventually takes off about 45 minutes late, to the sound of soul and jazz music on my headphones, into the dark West London skies.

We find ourselves eating our main meal of beef with green beans, at midnight UK time, but the food is enjoyable. Sylvia is struggling in the confined space, and I would say this is more so than before the Covid pandemic. Also, going to the toilet on the plane is a big challenge for Sylvia, directly due to her Parkinson's condition. She receives assistance in the toileting department from a delightful stewardess, who after learning about me, tells us she is desperate for a hip replacement. She also says that if we need anything, please ask her, as she has been allocated especially to assist Sylvia for the duration of the flight. I do my best to describe my recent hip replacement experience as positively as possible to her, and the stewardess seems encouraged. She also says she is amazed at Sylvia's resolve and determination to do the trip we are embarking upon.

We experience turbulence over the Bay of Bengal, and I watch a Julia Roberts weepie movie and an unedifying gangster film for a time. A curry meal is served at 05:00 UK time. It does seem strange to eat a hot curry when your body clock is telling you it is five in the morning!

Friday 17 February

Touching Down in Singapore

Our plane has made up the delay in taking off from Heathrow Airport, and touches down at Changi Airport in Singapore, on time, at 6:35 pm. It's been a generally smooth flight, although with a little turbulence here and there.

Changi Airport is modern, well looked after and well provided for in terms of amenities, and it has a light and airy feel about it. Sylvia remarks that she thinks the airport is a friendly place. I agree; I experience a friendly atmosphere to Changi Airport as well.

We realise quite quickly on landing that our two main cases have been transferred onto our flight to Cebu which takes off tomorrow, so we can't get access to them. In particular, we are concerned that Sylvia's wheelchair might have suffered the same fate. The assistance staff are quick to respond, however, and one of the pushers races off to the lost and found department and mercifully arrives back with our wheelchair. Massive crisis averted!

Our airport pusher, who tells us he is doing a nine-hour shift ending at 01:00 hrs tomorrow morning, takes us all the way to our hotel via the Sky Train. Although it is well into the evening, the temperature is still quite hot, at around 30 degrees Celsius, reflecting the fact that we are almost on the equator.

By the time we reach our hotel, at around nine o'clock, it is a dark night. We have been unexpectedly upgraded to luxury status, and our room is spacious and pleasant. The bed, however, sits quite high off the floor, which presents a challenge for Sylvia, but amazingly, somehow she manages to climb up onto it without mishap.

Saturday 18 February

Panicking in Singapore

As soon as I am awake, there is chaos and pandemonium in our bedroom as we experience a nightmare scenario. My mobile phone has run out of energy overnight and my alarm either didn't go off or I must have slept through it, both equally likely scenarios. From out of my sleepy torpor, I register with horror that the time on the bedside clock is nine o' clock, and it's immediately obvious that it's already highly likely that we are too late for us to get washed, medicated and dressed in time for breakfast. But my main initial worry is that we might not have sufficient time to make our flight to Cebu, which is scheduled to take off at 12:50 this afternoon.

The next hour is spent organising and administering Sylvia's tablets for the day ahead and then helping her get medicated, washed, dressed and organised, all at speed. At home, we usually have qualified carers to undertake this work, and it's something I always struggle with when the lot falls on me. Firstly, I take a two-minute shower, and I'm like a cat on a hot tin roof, wondering whether we really have left it too late to catch our flight on to Cebu in the Philippines. The consequences of that scenario don't bear thinking about.

Our sixth floor hotel bedroom window looks down directly onto the airport runway. But we have no time to admire the view. Eventually, we are ready to face the day and a guide calls at the hotel at 10:15 hours to take us via Sky Train to Terminal 2, to catch our flight to Cebu, passing the hotel's breakfast bar but with no time to stop there for anything to eat or drink. Sky Train seems to run on a magnetic strip, as opposed to conventional track.

Changi Airport is luxuriantly landscaped to a degree I haven't seen at an airport anywhere else, with a smattering of small parks, and vegetation is in profusion everywhere. There are also fountains and simulated waterfalls. It's all very impressive and exudes a satisfying, relaxing feel to the place.

There is time enough for us to wait in a business lounge, where we discover we can partake of a free breakfast (with lots of liquid intake) in convivial surroundings. So, we haven't missed out on a breakfast, after all!

Our wheelchair pusher to the departure gate is a guy called Neil, who says he was born and bred in Singapore. I say to him that the last time we were in Singapore was before he was born. "Welcome back!" he says, and offers to push me in a wheelchair as well as Sylvia. "It will be my gym session for the day!" he jokes. But I'm OK and I walk with my stick for 30 minutes or so, slowly but surely, to the appointed gate.

We are welcomed onto a relatively small Singapore Airlines aircraft with a central aisle and two seats on each row on either side. Good views are to be had from our seats. My camera comes into use for the first time on this holiday. Our plane is in a small queue of aircraft taxiing to the runway, which seems to be taking an age to sort out. But then, it is a busy airport. The pilot later apologises to the passengers for the long time it takes to finally take off from Singapore.

Immediately following take-off, we are flying over water and a series of inlets, some with ocean going ships at anchor. I am surprised at how green it all looks, although it is pockmarked by sites which look like they are clearly earmarked for development. The open sea has lines of shipping which are presumably waiting to gain entry to the port of Singapore, one of the busiest ports in the world. The clear, blue sky is punctuated by small, fluffy clouds. There is almost no turbulence, unlike a few sections of yesterday's flight.

I keep on trying to cram Japanese phrases into my tired brain. I have just about mastered "Do you speak English" at the fiftieth attempt. I then relax by listening to in-flight entertainment through the headphones provided by the airline, including BB King and then on to Bob Dylan's *Blood on the Tracks* and *Bringing it all back Home* albums. Face masks are obligatory on this flight.

A small island appears below the clouds. It's maybe half a mile long, although it is difficult to be precise from our height, with what appears to be a perfect beach and thick, virgin forest covering the rest of the island. Does anyone live there? I ask myself. But I can't see any obvious signs of human habitation. Several more islands of a similar size and character come into view before they are enveloped by mist and cloud. The Singapore Airlines air hostesses are all incredibly slim; it's almost unnatural.

Some of Bob Dylan's lyrics never fail to impress me, such as: "It's a wonder that you still know how to breathe"; and "You don't need a weather man to see which way the wind blows." Maybe they take me back to my halcyon student days, to a bygone era, when I actually bought a few Dylan records. But I can't remember ever having possession of a record player!

Our air hostess taps me on the shoulder and asks me about my camera. She says that she is very impressed that I am not using my mobile phone to take photographs! During our meal on the plane, strong turbulence hits the plane in the middle of the dessert course, but it doesn't last for too long. And I am certainly not passing up on my dessert!

We clip what I think must be the north coast of Borneo. The landscape comprises thick forests and muddy inlets and rivers. A couple of meandering rivers have produced a few ox-bow lakes. Several small settlements appear, generally located on the banks of the waterways.

Further on, we fly over the large southern Philippine island of Mindanao, one of the biggest in the entire (and extensive) Philippines archipelago. It is mountainous and carpeted in dark green forest. A few rivers cut their way impressively through the island's topography in incised meanders. The settlement pattern is mainly focused on ribbon development along many of the roads.

We come down to land at Davao, the principal settlement on the island of Mindanao. In addition to shanty towns, there are affluent looking neighbourhoods, and rush hour traffic jams can be seen as we approach five o'clock in the early evening.

We all have to disembark at Davao Airport – everyone except for Sylvia, that is, who is given special dispensation on account of her disability. This provides an army of cleaners the opportunity to tidy up the plane. In the airport complex, I notice a couple of shrines to St Joseph. Several ladies are kneeling at these statues and kissing them, but no men are doing this as far as I can see.

Shortly after taking off from Davao, generally reckoned to be the second largest urban area in the Philippines, the city's sea port comes into view. It has separate zones for modern shipping and also areas set aside for traditional craft, where there appears to be a lot of fishing vessels. But then we fly over another section of coast which is reserved for modern shipping, and further along, back to traditional vessels, creating something representing a piano keyboard effect. It looks like the traditional port areas can't be bought out that easily by the new kids on the block, so everyone has to live almost cheek by jowl as close neighbours. We notice this 'cheek by jowl' mentality later on when we explore Cebu city.

Soon we are experiencing an impressive sunset, with thin horizontal layers of cloud breaking up the red glow of the sun, with further layers of white clouds below. The Salvador Dali effect is broken up by heavy rain beating down, but after a while the clouds below us glow red from the sun, and it creates a sublime, almost ethereal effect.

By six-twenty it is all dark outside the plane, except for a straight, continuous red glow on the horizon. The rain has ceased, and the pilot announces that the temperature is currently 25 degrees Celsius in Cebu.

Cebu city comes into view, comprising a mass of lights along the waterfront, with a long bridge stretching out from the city to some point underneath the plane, making the bridge even more mysterious. A huge, luminous, yellow sign advertising a McDonald's eatery catches my eye.

We touch down in the evening rain in Cebu city. However, it feels pleasantly warm. Everyone at the airport is friendly, even though I haven't completed a necessary entry form. Fortunately, an official completes it for me, although this takes half an hour. Sylvia is attended to by a posse of cleaners, waiting to access the plane; she is truly the centre of attention. We are almost the last of the passengers to enter the arrivals hall, where we spot our son Nathan and his fiancée Melodie, who tell us they were beginning to wonder whether we would ever make it off the plane.

It's our first time seeing Nathan in three years and it's been nearly five years since we last saw Melodie. I am getting pretty emotional as I set eyes on them in the arrivals hall, which takes me a little by surprise. After hugs, etc., we are introduced to Kang, a young Filipino lady who has agreed to assist Sylvia as her carer over the next few days. She will be our constant companion during our time in Cebu city.

We make our way out of the airport and clamber on board a people carrier that Nathan and Melodie have booked. Somehow we manage to get Sylvia out of her wheelchair and up into the vehicle. It takes us through crowded streets, full of people as well as vehicular traffic, to our hotel. Even in the rain, the crowded streets are busy with human activity, but there again, this is warm rain, more 'people friendly' than the colder rain that we experience in more temperate latitudes. We drive quite a way, probably for several miles, and I form the impression that this city spreads out extensively.

Our destination, the Bai Hotel, Cebu, rises above its urban neighbours like a colossus. It is about 23 storeys high. We make our way to our room – or rooms - which comprise a lounge in addition to a bedroom and a fully accessible bathroom. It's very spacious and ideal for us, and especially for Sylvia. We all set to work to help Sylvia get sorted out and settled in, and at around nine o'clock the four of us make our way down to the main restaurant in the hotel.

I ask Nathan about he and Melodie getting used to each other after a period of over three years of living apart physically, due to the Covid restrictions on travel. Melodie responds by saying that the main difference is that Nathan is now within punching distance! Melodie says that she had to remind herself continually in the first few days that Nathan was physically with her or near her. It is testament to their mutual commitment which is to be cemented in a few days' time that they have survived as an 'item' having been physically apart from each other for so long.

Our meal in the hotel is buffet-style. Nathan and Melodie introduce us to local specialities, including curries, squid and shrimp. After dinner, Nathan and Melodie continue to help to organise us. It's almost midnight when they say goodbye and we then enjoy a good night's sleep.

Sunday 19 February

Getting to know Cebu

The hotel phone ejects me from sleep mode by ringing at 07:45 hrs.; the receptionist on the other end of the line tells me that our new carer, Kang, has arrived in the hotel lobby. I dash into the bathroom, put on a towel and let Kang in to our bedroom. She quickly gets to work on introducing Sylvia to the new day.

By 09:30 we are all ready to descend to level 2 in the hotel for breakfast. An army of masked helpers attends to our culinary needs. The breakfast area is heaving with customers and waitresses and waiters attending to them. I am disorientated at first with so many people. But a kindly steward notices my crutch and general state of confusion and offers to get anything I want. The hotel staff can't do enough to help us; we are almost overrun with politeness and a desire to give us assistance.

I observe quite a few tall white guys or just plain big white guys, many of whom appear to be North American, judging by their accents, accompanied by diminutive, young Filipino ladies. Nathan says that this is a common phenomenon in this part of the world.

We gain extensive views of the city, looking out of our twelfth floor bedroom window. Given that it is a Sunday in a deeply Catholic country, it is not surprising that there is little traffic on the streets, although there is some shipping on the move, to and from the port of Cebu.

A large body of water is visible between our part of the city and a separate urban area on the far shore. The land between the hotel and the waterfront comprises a mixture of industrial and warehousing plots, including a container storage park right below the hotel. There are several quays for shipping, including for ferries, whilst there are pockets of shanty town housing, mostly with tin roofs and packed in to relatively small plots at a great density, in 'cheek by jowl' fashion. One dreads what would happen in the event of a fire in these shanty areas.

In other directions, away from the waterway, there are apartment blocks and some pockets of low-rise housing, set against a mountainous backdrop. What looks like another hotel, or a set of apartment blocks, is under construction on a nearby plot; this new development is blocking out part of the panoramic view of the waterway from our bedroom. However, it is almost universal in planning law that there is no right to a view.

I decide to go for a walk/wheelchair push down to the waterside, but a guy in the hotel reception says this is: "Not for the people", which could be translated as: "Not for the tourists". Then, a security guard advises that we go for a walk later, maybe around 4 pm, as it is too hot now (12:30 pm). There are no obvious pedestrian routes that I can find from the hotel, and it is an area where the motor car reigns supreme. So, we settle for drinks in a café (the Wall Street Bar) on the edge of the hotel compound. The waiter informs us that Cebu city centre is about an hour away in heavy traffic, and this gives me some idea about the size of the urban area of this city.

Nathan arrives in the early afternoon, and our aim is to walk to the nearby shopping mall. But the first (and only as far as we can find) disabled ramp is almost impossible for the wheelchair to negotiate, being far too steep and flimsy, and then there are no further disabled ramps that we can see in any direction. Defeat is experienced again at another attempt to escape from our hotel on foot/wheelchair.

Whilst we are looking for disabled access ramps in the vicinity, Nathan is approached by a young girl for money. We spot a controlling 'mama' on the opposite side of the road, who is sending out half a dozen or so kids on money-making missions. There is an awkward juxtaposition in this area between the economic 'haves' and the 'have nots'.

The light rain makes the temperature quite pleasant, aided and abetted by a pronounced breeze. We end up back in the same coffee bar as earlier in the day, but we make sure to avoid the sickly, sugary, diabetes-inducing drink I had before, when I mistakenly thought it was a mango smoothie!

Tiredness is beginning to kick in after our long flights of a few days ago; I keep on nodding off and wrecking a message I am trying to send on my mobile phone to one of our Japanese friends, Kyoko, regarding our visit to Kyoto in a few weeks' time.

Later in the afternoon, we meet up with Melodie, and we all take a taxi ride to a nearby shopping mall. Sylvia buys some mosquito repellent, as she has already been bitten several times. My blood is obviously not good enough for them, which is fine by me, and so far I have got away with virtually no bites.

We dine out at a Persian kebabs restaurant within the same shopping area, but none of us has a full appetite. Melodie takes all the spare meat off our plates to feed the stray dogs, of which there are many, once she is out of sight of the restaurant.

It's back to our hotel for an early night, which we really need.

Monday 20 February

Historic Cebu

Nathan and Melodie collect us from our hotel mid-morning and the four of us take a taxi to the downtown area of Cebu city. On our way, we travel past an extensive docks area, maybe covering over a mile of cranes and wharfs. Apparently, the Mayor of Cebu is on record as saying that his ambition for Cebu city is to make it into another Singapore. If he is successful in achieving this aim, he will need to do something about the huge deficit in provision for disabled access, in which it is currently streets, or is it continents, behind Singapore, in fact on a different planet.

We alight from our taxi in Magellan Square in the heart of the city's historic core, where a number of traditional buildings mix with more contemporary structures. But the building heights are relatively low, which seems to be controlled by the city's planners, and even the fascia treatment of the local McDonald's restaurant is subdued. So, some provision has been put into place by the city authorities towards conserving its important heritage.

We walk through an open area of gardens to a small dome-like structure which houses a cross – aptly named Magellan's Cross, dated 1521 – which is said to be the original cross given to the locals by the great Portuguese explorer, Ferdinand Magellan, who was heading an expedition of exploration on behalf of the King of Spain. The story of Magellan's visit is told pictorially on frescoes on the ceiling of the structure.

Close by Magellan's Cross, is the Basilica de Santo Niño (Spanish for 'Holy Child'), which is a church dating back to the early days of the Spanish colonial period. We sit down in the cool in one of the pews of the church, which is a welcome respite from the heat outside. This is part of a religious complex, with a cathedral next door. An image of the Baby Jesus was brought by Magellan, but within a month of this meeting, he had been killed at the nearby Battle of Mactan by a local Moslem chief called Lapu Lapu.

The Spanish constructed their biggest fort in the Philippines at Cebu, and it's our next port of call. The Fort San Pedro, dating from 1565, is a bulky and impressive artefact, which looks down on the rest of the city, from a position of dominance. Its sheer bulk was probably there to instil a measure of fear or a sense of awe upon the local inhabitants of Cebu. At the time when it was built, it extended to the sea shore, although there has been significant land reclamation over the intervening centuries. It takes the appearance of a huge, stone three-cornered hat, defined by its three apexes. As we walk through the entrance, we are serenaded by a trio playing Beatles numbers, which comes as a slight culture shock to me.

The fort has been beautifully landscaped and the stonework of its ramparts is attractive, and conveys a sense of permanency. In one corner of the fort there is a well which was used to house prisoners, who, so our guide tells us, were drowned when the sea level rose with the incoming tide.

We get chatting to some Taiwanese tourists in the fort. One of them says that his son is studying at Kings College, London. When I ask him what subject he is reading at King's, he replies: "I don't know – I just pay!"

The heat is intense as we walk and push the wheelchair along all three sides of the fort and get some idea of how this structure would have dominated the local settlement. The temperature, at around 35 degrees Celsius, is significantly hotter than yesterday.

From atop the fort, the sprawling urban mass of Cebu city extends in all directions. Wealthy houses are located in close proximity to flimsy wooden structures, which sometimes, precariously, rise to the height of three storeys plus. There is also a phenomenal mixture of roadside uses, often with direct vehicular access to the main highways.

We stop for a meal of grilled fish at a local eating establishment, which we are informed, is a genuine Filipino restaurant. We secure a table near to an air fan, which turns out to be a good move. The place has a noisy and vivacious atmosphere, but has a relaxed feeling nonetheless. Phil Collins – or rather a recording of him – is singing over the general hubbub. It's an oasis from the busy city and from where we are seated, it's quite breezy and pleasant. We also enjoy our grilled fish!

After lunch, we are taken to Melodie's family home, situated in the outskirts of the city. It is a gated community, with several dwellings accommodating different members of the extended family. Melodie's mother's home has a balcony which seems to be a popular meeting place, as much for dogs as humans; there are several puppies around six weeks old, all wanting to be made a fuss of (eight in all), so Sylvia is in her element. The puppies' home is a large cardboard box, into which several holes have been cut to enable them to see the world outside. We are quite amused by this, seeing their little faces peering out of these windows. Sylvia, however, conks out for more than 40 winks for a while, as jet lag gets the better of her. The family home has a pleasant backdrop of trees and an outhouse which seems to be well used as a meeting place/games area.

Sylvia and I are introduced to Melodie's mom, Leticia, who welcomes us to her home. She is not backward in firstly telling me her age, which is 67 years, and follows on from this, by telling me that she is looking for a new husband, and can I help? So, I have a new mission when I return to the UK! We are also introduced to Melodie's daughter, whom everybody calls KC, and who quite understandably is less forthcoming than her grandmother, in fact, quite the reverse.

KC shows me round the compound, which is home to the extended family. But outside in the yard area, I trip over a stool and draw blood. Leticia and Melodie work overtime to clean up my wound and apply a plaster, and I am certainly in good hands. However, the dogs like the idea of licking my sore (or trying to). On the way back from walking round the compound, I accidently push open the wrong door, to KC's uncle's house! But we get away without causing a major incident. Melodie then shows us her wedding dress, which is still a work in progress, with the wedding in three days' time!

The neighbourhood surrounding the family compound looks to have been developed organically, with a cacophony of building styles and materials, and with lots of people standing around along the main road and chatting. As we depart to go back to the hotel at around eight o'clock in the evening, everybody still seems to be out on the streets, and there are dozens of small shops, cafes, workshops and other facilities open and seemingly doing a brisk trade. Motorcycles compete with cars, trucks, buses, taxis and pedal cycles for road space; there are lots of near misses but no accidents that I can see. Our taxi driver, however, is a skilful manoeuvrer, and I have nothing but respect for the way he handles the pressures of the traffic around him.

Back at the hotel, I make contact with one of our Japanese students, Fujio, whom we will be spending time with when we get to Japan in March. It is good to see him on my mobile phone screen, and we tell him we have booked into a hotel in Hiroshima.

Tuesday 21 February

Projects and Plans

As usual, we are immersed or even smothered in kindness the minute we step into the breakfast area of our hotel. Our special breakfast steward is called Merry, and she impressively remembers all the culinary items I asked for yesterday. I ask her where I can buy a map of Cebu city, and she tells me she will buy one and give it to me at breakfast tomorrow. She also refuses to take any money for doing this. So, I plan to retaliate and give her one of my books.

Over breakfast I ask Kang, if she has a choice of countries to visit, where would she choose?

"Canada" she says.

"Why?" I ask.

"Because it's a good place to earn money as a care giver", she replies.

So, whereas my question is framed to her as a tourist, Kang's mentality is based on her need to make money, so as to make ends meet; Kang is desperate to leave the Philippines just to survive economically. If necessary, she says, she would leave her son behind in the care of her mother and go it alone. This practice seems to be commonplace in the Philippines, and we have come across examples of it back in the UK.

There is a container storage area immediately below the hotel, and we have a direct view of it from our bedroom window. A single crane is lifting one container at a time and mostly loading them onto waiting lorries. Two men perch, somewhat precariously, on top of each container which is about to be lifted and moved by the crane; they are hanging onto ropes to help them keep their balance. Once the containers are in the air, the men often swing about as though they are on a choppy sea. A lorry is loaded every two minutes or so, with a line of them which are waiting to be loaded, and in a few cases, unloaded. The depot is a hive of activity. It starts to rain, making the surfaces of the containers slippery and the work of the men on top of them even more precarious, but the work carries on regardless.

In the afternoon, we make it to the hotel pool bar on the twenty-first floor of our hotel. A central island, with dining tables and chairs, is flanked by two slender pools. Relaxing jazz music can be heard in the background. From the few amorous couples who are up here, I think I detect spoken Russian. Rain is falling into the pools. Extensive views of Cebu city include the port area and the new Mactan Bridge, which is a long, slender and graceful structure. The clouds have descended to a level below the mountainous backdrop to the city.

On the opposite side of the pool bar, the view extends to the sea, including the mouth of the passage of water separating the island of Cebu from Mactan, and the other two bridges joining the islands. There are also views down onto several small shanty settlements, where their interiors seem to be almost impenetrable. The buildings and structures appear to be ridiculously tightly crammed together, with mostly one and two storey tin roofs (some tiled).

In between taking photographs from the twenty-first floor, I get chatting to a friendly Canadian guy who is writing on a notepad. I ask him if he is a fellow travel writer. He replies that he writes journals to God. Well, I did ask him.

Nathan drops by later in the afternoon. He has just had his hair cut, and looks quite posh, in preparation for his big day on 23 February. We take a taxi to a local shopping mall (Park Mall) where we look for a raincoat for Sylvia. We are unsuccessful, having scoured the entire mall. We settle for an early evening meal of noodles, vegetables and spicy meat. Again, it's really hot eating our meal at seven in the evening in a very crowded place.

Also in the mall, there is a model of the proposed development of the apartment block that we can see under construction from our hotel bedroom. It is to be known as City Clou. I am handed a leaflet, welcoming me to Cebu's first ever Community Business District. Our hotel is conspicuous in its absence from the map in the brochure, even though it is clearly within this area. Given that the emerging City Clou has wiped out a significant proportion of the view over the waterway from our hotel, I can imagine that there is no love lost between the two companies.

The map showing the Community Business District is also silent on the existence of several shanty towns and their planned future. And, I wonder, are there also plans to relocate the very active container storage depot which is located directly between our hotel and City Clou? Does the project address the huge issue of disabled accessibility in and around the neighbourhood, which, to put it mildly, is not joined up or even approaching being joined up, in what currently could be described as Petrol Head City?

Wednesday 22 February

Of Mice and Men

True to her word, our waitress, Merry, greets us at our breakfast table with a map, which she says she bought last night for me, as promised. However, it is a political map of the Philippines at a small scale, not a street map of Cebu which is what I am after. I haven't the heart to tell her that I had asked for a different map and thank her for her efforts. But the map does inform me that Cebu city has over four million inhabitants, possibly second only to the Greater Manilla conurbation in the Philippines. In exchange, I give her one of my books, which is well received.

Merry chats to us about her way of life. She says she gets up at two o'clock in the morning, to arrive at work by 05:00 hrs. She also tells us that she has a pet dragon, which makes a noise which acts as her early morning alarm! In addition, she has a cat and a dog. Apparently, they all get on well with each other, which I guess is an absolute must.

We arrange to hire a driver through the hotel reception – a guy named Paul to be precise. He pops up from reception to our room and runs through the possibilities with us. My idea of crossing the island to a place called Toledo is met with comments that the place has a copper mine and builds ships, i.e. it is hardly a suitable place to visit as a tourist (I personally wouldn't have minded!). So, we opt for Plan B – to visit Busai Gardens, up in the mountains in the centre of the island.

Paul tells us that the shanty towns we can see from the hotel are occupied by squatters. One of these areas was created recently after a convention centre mysteriously burnt down. The Government, so we are informed, offered the squatters relocation areas, but these were considered too far away from where the jobs are, and the squatters therefore rejected the Government's offers. And, he adds, the Government has no power to dispossess them.

We order a taxi to take us to SM Seaside shopping mall, situated close to the city centre. It is a huge new mall, on the scale of the Trafford Centre or Lakeside back in the UK. The place burns a hole in my pocket, as Sylvia comes away with an expensive, but light weight, attractive dark blue rain jacket, which she loves. She now feels she is ready to take on the rigours of Japan in a few days time.

We call in at a coffee bar within the mall, with the unimaginative title of Coffee Bay. Its strap line is: *Roasting on a dream at a time* – 'Roasting on a mortgage at a time' might have been more appropriate, judging by their prices, and they don't accept cash. But at least the coffee is half decent.

Driving to and from the SM Seaside mall, we pass by the new bridge to Mactan Island. It really is a superbly gracious structure, which sweeps curvaceously over us with the sea on one side and the city on the other.

The designer coffee gets its revenge on me by late afternoon, leaving me sitting on the toilet for ages. It also starts raining, which pours from thick black clouds, indicating the wet stuff is here to stay. This knocks the trip to the mountainous restaurant on the head. Instead, it's an early night in at our hotel.

Thursday 23 February

The Wedding

This is the day we thought would never happen. Nathan is finally getting married! He comes over to our hotel mid-morning, along with a guy called Justin, who is introduced as a family friend. Nathan seems quite relaxed and even makes a few quips. I think we are more nervous than he is! (And I certainly was a lot more nervous at our wedding, over half a century ago!)

Justin drives Sylvia, Nathan and me for an hour and a half through the burgeoning metropolis of Cebu city to the wedding venue. Almost every section of the highway network we drive along is congested, and it is a hot, sunny day.

The wedding venue Nathan and Melodie have chosen is situated in the Banawa District of Cebu city. It is a colonial looking building, with moderately extensive grounds, which goes by the name of La Casa Vieja (Spanish for 'The Old House'), although I am not sure it is old enough for the Spanish colonialists to have built it. La Casa Vieja's main building may not look that ancient, but it has a pleasant, informal courtyard, and also a long balcony. It apparently was the ancestral home of a Filipino/Spanish family. The courtyard is flanked by a couple of banana trees and other tropical vegetation. It is an oasis of calm in this bustling city of an estimated four million souls, and as we have arrived early, we have some time to take in our surroundings, at our own pace, as it were.

The building opposite accommodates life-sized statues of Mary and Joseph (two of the central characters in the Christian Nativity story) in its front garden and the access to the wedding venue appears to turn into a country lane beyond the venue, leading to a few fields in the distance through the heat haze. It is a pleasant if warm day for the wedding, with the temperature around 31 degrees Celsius. Butterflies waft, cockerels screech and a few barking dogs can be heard in this semi-rural inlier in the city.

The wedding ceremony for Nathan and his wife-to-be Melodie is scheduled to begin at 3pm, but everyone is informally chatting and taking photographs at this official start time. A formal start to the proceedings is delayed until 4:15, and it is taking place in the grounds just outside the house. Mercifully, there is a small breeze. Nathan is amused by one of Melodie's friends, who, upon seeing Melodie in her car, wearing all her wedding finery (which, by the way, she designed and made herself, and only completed late last night), remarks to her: "Melodie, you look beautiful, just like your mother!" I have it on good authority that the person issuing that remark got thumped.

A small guy steps forward and the wedding ceremony starts. What he says is simple and profound. This in itself is a shock to Sylvia and I, who were expecting a secular piece of bureaucracy, and we had steeled ourselves for that outcome. We then discover, immediately after the service, that the guy leading it is an evangelical bishop in the Philippine church; Sylvia and I experience a lot of joy when we make this discovery.

During the wedding service, the bishop takes about five minutes delivering his message, based on the acrostic ACTS, which I think stand for admiration, commitment, teachability and sacrifice. He quotes from Christian Scripture (1 Corinthians 13 to be precise), and I think he catches Nathan out at one point (Nathan, who has aimed not to say anything by way of a speech during the entire ceremony), by asking him to say, publicly, a few words to his new wife. It seems to take Nathan a few seconds to process this, but he does say something appropriate in the end. It's the nearest Nathan gets to delivering a speech the entire day.

After a few prayers and some music (part Christian in genre plus a few classics of popular songs, including at least one Elvis hit), a few mainly short speeches or tributes emanate from the audience, or can we now call it a congregation?

Then the buffet meal advertises its existence through a pleasant aroma wafting down from inside the Casa Vieja kitchen. People are mindful of our disabilities, and both Sylvia and I have our meals served directly to us.

It's good to see that Nathan is clearly on good terms with Melodie's family and he works the room (or should it be referred to as the grounds) very well. Several of Melodie's friends and relatives come up to us and introduce themselves. These include Melodie's sister, Jo Anne and her husband Raul, a lawyer, who are very welcoming and chatty. We end up inviting them over to the UK at some point in the future, and we really hope they will be able to make it.

When it comes to the toasts, someone remarks that the toast to the bride and groom will be given by the groom's father. "That's me!" I remark, as a microphone is thrust into my hand! Doubtless to everyone's relief, I don't speak for too long.

Several guests come over and chat to us and we are made to feel extremely welcome throughout the entire day. It has turned into a lovely party.

By the end of the partying and socialising, I think we have managed to get around to inviting half of the assembled host back to our place in the UK for a holiday (let's hope they don't all arrive at the same time), and the bride's mother has repeated her commission for me to find her a man from somewhere, anywhere.

We arrange to meet up with Nathan and Melodie at midday tomorrow and, shortly after darkness falls, Justin, our family friend, drives us back to our hotel. It has been a wonderful day.

Friday 24 February

Plantation Bay

We need to arrange for a Covid PCR test for Sylvia, or she won't be going to Japan (and neither will I!). However, the hospital nearest to our next hotel, on the island of Mactan, no longer does PCR tests. I also enquire at our current hotel reception for a place to get the test done. They ring around, find one place where the PCR equipment has been removed and can't get through to two other places. We therefore agree to call in at the Cebu Doctors' Hospital, the main hospital in the city, this afternoon. Even within the hospital complex, the signs to the test centre are vague.

Over breakfast, we get in touch with one of our Japanese contacts – and friend – Tomoru, over WhatsApp. He is currently at a convention in Tokyo. It will be good to see him again and touch base. He will be our companion and guide for a couple of days in and around Tokyo next month.

I spend some of the morning reading John Le Carré's latest – and last – novel, *Silverview*. This is the story that had to be completed by others.

Nathan and Melodie arrive at our hotel at about 12:30 hrs and we then check out. For the next few days, the four of us will be staying on the neighbouring Island of Mactan, at the Plantation Bay Hotel or Resort. Part of me feels like an imposter, being with the happy couple on the first few days of their honeymoon, but it was their idea! Our taxi driver taking us to our new hotel uses the new bridge joining Cebu to Mactan that we looked down upon on our flight from Singapore, about a week ago. Mactan Island accommodates the airport and has several beach resort hotels, including the one we are aiming for. Much of the island is still green fields, but it appears to be developing fast.

The Plantation Bay Hotel Resort where we are staying for a few days comprises a set of well-spaced out apartments spread around a salt water lagoon, whilst the south-east side of the complex borders the sea, including having a sandy beach. It is set within an ambience of whispering palms, and we experience the refreshing feel of being far from the madding crowd. It is an excellent place for Nathan and Melodie to chill after all the activity and stresses of planning for and arranging their wedding.

The need for a PCR for Sylvia is very much on my mind, and as soon as we arrive at our resort hotel – Plantation Bay – out of desperation, I ask the person on reception if he can recommend anywhere to do the test. He says they have a nurse on site who would be able to undertake this, and he calls for her. This is really unexpected and welcome good news.

As we are waiting for the nurse at reception, we get chatting to a lady by the name of Esther, originally from these parts, and her English husband, Graham. They live in Salisbury in the UK and met through an agency for bringing together grieving partners (or ex-partners). The organisation has clearly worked out well for them!

Our apartment has good wheelchair access and a balcony overlooking the lagoon. It's just a few steps down to the grassy sward and then onto the sand fringing the lagoon. Nathan and Melodie are located in an apartment quite near to us. Our accommodation has house rules in English, Chinese, Japanese, Korean and Russian.

At around three-thirty, the four of us set off for a small late lunch, over which we start to relax. Nathan and Melodie seem to be very natural with each other; Sylvia and I feel privileged that they have included us in what is effectively the first day of their honeymoon.

My recurring nightmare in this holiday is the sheer amount (and weight) of stuff we are taking with us, especially when we will be on our own for much of our time in Japan. Then, late in the afternoon, I get a brainwave (well, it is one by my standards). Why not take some large carrier bags with us to Japan, leave them at our first hotel in Tokyo, full of stuff we no longer need for the rest of our travels, and then collect them on the last day of our holiday when we will be staying overnight at the same hotel in Tokyo? Is this a stroke of genius or a statement of the blinkin' obvious?

After our (very) late lunch, we make it to the beach. Across a few miles of sea, we can make out the hills of the neighbouring Philippines island of Bohol, where Nathan and Melodie have bought two plots of land, apparently both about the size of a couple of tennis courts, for development at some unidentified point (as of now) in the future. A possible trip if we ever come out here again? I ask myself.

We crash out in the late afternoon before the four of us meet up for a meal in one of the four restaurants in the complex. One thing I am learning about Melodie is that she is keen to share her food. It reveals a giving trait in her character.

We enjoy a relatively early night.

Saturday 25 February

The Swab Test

I wake up in the early hours and find it difficult to get back to sleep. So, I read a chapter of my Le Carré novel, which is starting to come together after about a hundred pages; this is about par for the course with his books, in my experience.

At a reasonable hour in the morning, Sylvia and I make our way to the Kilimanjaro Restaurant, which is situated over the lagoon and is approached via a wooden bridge with slats, resembling a gangplank. We enjoy our breakfast and after half an hour we are joined by the honeymoon couple, both of whom look remarkably chilled out.

We have booked the Covid PCR swab test for Sylvia, and it is to be carried out at a hospital near to the Bai Hotel in Cebu city, where we were last week. After some nervous waiting, a taxi driver arrives and we think we will be lucky to make it in time for our appointment at 1:30 pm. Our fears are compounded by the sheer congestion on the highways. Vehicles continuously barge in and cyclists run rings around us, amounting to total mayhem.

Eventually, on the third attempt, the drive-in CPR test area is identified by the taxi driver. Even in the hospital complex, there are no direction signs to guide drivers to the actual test area. We arrive late, but everyone is relaxed about this, and the process is painless for Sylvia, although painful on the wallet. But at least we are now on the way to get our access to Japan. Sylvia's test results are to be emailed back to our resort on Monday, i.e. within 72 hours of our departure for Japan, in accordance with the regulations. This looks like mission accomplished.

The island of Mactan still is home to substantial green areas with a profusion of tropical vegetation. Many people carry out their businesses from the roadside, resulting in a lot of impromptu parking, conflicting traffic manoeuvres and near misses. They would get short shrift from British highway engineers, or they would give them a heart attack!

Back at the resort complex, Nathan and I make our way together – in my case very gingerly – into the salt water lagoon, which is located close to our chalet. Although we are minding our own business, just talking to each other, in a quiet tone of voice, we become engaged in conversation by a young boy, maybe ten years old, who seems, in my view at least, to be quite advanced along the autism scale. He chips in quite a few times into the middle of our conversation. On one occasion he asks us what are we talking about. Nathan replies with: "Politics", which throws him completely, and he eventually gets bored with our company. Nathan and I remain in the lagoon until it gets dark, and we must have spent at least an hour relaxing and chatting in the most laid back of surroundings.

As we emerge from the water, Melodie and her daughter KC join us in our chalet. KC will spend a couple of days with us before she and her mother go their separate ways. (Melodie will be taking on a new job in Dubai, whilst KC will continue with her studies in Cebu.)

The five of us experience a great meal tonight – Malaysian sea food curry, with just the right degree of spiciness. We are in bed fairly early tonight.

Sunday 26 February

Remembering Lapu Lapu

Seeing as it's a Sunday, Sylvia and I hold an impromptu local service, just the two of us, looking at Psalm 84, where it says that even the birds have a special place in creation. At a more mundane level, we discover that our swimming kit has completely dried out overnight. This looks like turning into another hot day, with no sign of approaching rain. I could seriously get used to this!

The lagoon is being cleaned today, to remove detritus resulting from recent heavy rainfall. The water level in the lagoon is significantly lower than yesterday. Any noise on this Sunday morning is even more subdued than usual and we are caught up with the wind rustling through the palm trees which encircle the lagoon.

The four of us hire a taxi to take us to a memorial on the island, to a character named Lapu Lapu, who was the local tribesman who killed Magellan at the Battle of Mactan in 1521. Our driver, Jonathan, is welcoming and friendly, and we become companions for the next couple of hours. He tells us he used to work as a truck driver, taking pharmaceutical supplies over to the neighbouring island of Negros, to the west of Cebu. He started driving taxis in 2017 rather than some other better paid jobs because, as he says, he likes meeting people and making friends. And he certainly likes meeting people!

The site of the Battle of Mactan is today a largely concreted over, extensive pedestrian area and it lies next to a reed-fringed waterway leading to the sea. On the 'inland' side of the historic battlefield site, a development is being proclaimed on huge signs as

'Mactan New Town'. A few high-rise developments (15 or so storeys high) are towering above land occupied by squatters.

The statue of Lapu Lapu shows a huge and fit, muscular guy with what looks like a surfboard (probably a shield) and I imagine Magellan was no match for him in combat. Another monument close by celebrates the glory of Spain and the joint monarchy of Ferdinand and Isabella, who basically brought Spain together into one united nation and a leading world power at the time. Looking at a large wall painting of the battle on display, it is clear that Magellan's men were heavily outnumbered by the local forces. Whilst looking at the picture, Nathan says to Jonathan: "All this happened a long time ago – my dad was only nine at the time!" Jonathan looks confused and says he doesn't understand. Another one of Nathan's jokes bites the dust.

Although Mactan Island has a more relaxed feel than Cebu City, the impact of the airport and the recent bridge construction is leading to increased traffic congestion – or "very traffic" as many of the islanders would say. There are still rural backwaters on the island, where shacks and other informal structures appear half-buried beneath a carpet of vegetation. But the march of progress across the island continues, seemingly unabated.

Jonathan, our friendly taxi driver, is keen to take us to the airport on Tuesday morning, when we will fly to Tokyo. He is even keen to collect us from our resort at the anti-social time of 04:30 hours.

Jonathan drives us to part of the island known as Cordova on the north coast of Mactan, where we discover a restaurant situated on a wooden platform facing out to sea, with the outline of the island of Bohol in the distance. Several fishing boats are tied up to the restaurant decking. I hope my camera takes a good photograph of a lone canoeist crossing the sparkling water reflecting the late afternoon sun; to the naked eye, it certainly looks photogenic. We order mango juice, but without any sugar, milk or ice cream, which initially is met with incredulity by the waiter. But the bar staff come up with a simplified mango drink, which goes down well with us.

Back at the resort, Nathan and I go swimming around seven in the evening in one of the fresh water pools, where we also discover a secluded jacuzzi. In the dark, Nathan assists me along a narrow causeway with the aid of his mobile phone torch. Once in the pool, which is illuminated, the water reassuringly takes my weight and I can relax. We spend around half an hour chilling out, this time with no strangers gate-crashing in on our conversation.

Around eight o'clock, the four of us, plus Melodie's daughter KC, meet for an evening meal in Kilimanjaro Restaurant. I try a Korean speciality, based on marinated beef, which is very enjoyable.

KC has to go to school tomorrow, where she is involved in a project on educational standards in the Philippines. Nathan and Melodie take her home to Cebu City and then aim to return to Plantation Bay Resort tonight. Sylvia and I just retire to bed.

Monday 27 February

Calamity Strikes

At around three in the morning, I take Sylvia in her wheelchair to use the facilities, so to speak. On attempting to clamber back onto the bed, Sylvia falls, and I struggle unsuccessfully to lift her off the floor. In the end, I call the help line, whereupon six substantially sized men troop into our bedroom, but even they can't lift Sylvia to the height of the bed (its height being the cause of the problem). Finally, one of the men suggests that we move into the next door accommodation, which fortuitously happens to be vacant, and which has a significantly lower bed. We accept this suggestion.

Our problems, however, don't end there; Sylvia falls again around seven o'clock in the morning, trying to sit on a chair. This time, Nathan and Melodie come over and help. The delay means that we only just manage to make breakfast on time. This morning, traditional Filipino cuisine is on offer, so we are especially glad to have made it before closing time.

Later in the morning, Nathan and Melodie help us with our packing, ready for our departure tomorrow. Shortly after their arrival, the heavens open – there is thunder, lightning and crashing tropical rain for several hours. A good time to get stuck into my Le Carré novel, me thinks.

The nurse and her assistant visit us in the early afternoon, with the good news that Sylvia has tested negative to Covid, with a paper copy to prove it when we pass through Japanese security tomorrow. One more bit of paper for my travel folder!

Later, Nathan phones and says he has some work to complete this afternoon, and we all arrange to escape from the resort for dinner this evening.

It's our last meal together, and we decide to eat in a crowded eatery in the nearby Mactan New Town. Despite its name, in reality, it's more akin to a New High Street than a New Town. We order a variety of curries and fish dishes. Ubiquitous cats wander under our table as we dine. I've never encountered such friendly felines!

Nathan buys some bananas for Sylvia at one of the many roadside stores that we pass by on our way back to our resort.

Final farewells are undertaken once we are back in the resort, and we are in bed by ten o'clock, ready for a very early start in the morning.

Magellan's Cross, Cebu City

Basilica de Santo Niño, Cebu City

Fort San Pedro, Cebu City

Roadside properties, Cebu City

View of Cebu City from our hotel

Mactan Bridge

The evangelical bishop of the Philippines conducting the wedding

Nathan and Melodie's wedding, Cebu City

Plantation Bay Resort, Mactan Island

Plantation Bay Resort

Plantation Bay

Our driver, Jonathan, with Nathan and Sylvia

Statue of Lapu Lapu

A Walk on the Wild Side

View from restaurant, Cordova, Mactan Island

Lone canoeist, off Cordova

Mactan Bridge

Local Shop, Mactan Island

Tuesday 28 February

A long day travelling to Tokyo

My alarm goes off at the unearthly hour of 03:30 hrs, and it's a race to have everything ready by four-thirty, when Jonathan our taxi driver is due to arrive. We sort out our final bill with the resort at four o'clock, and the ever-cheerful Jonathan collects us on time, well, not that far off, at 04:40 hrs. He tells us he will be our taxi driver the next time we come to the Philippines! Absolutely no problem there!

Even on our journey to the airport, which takes the best part of an hour, there's a lot of traffic ("many traffic") on the dark streets of Mactan Island. Many people need to be up and about their business at this early hour. In addition to cars and bicycles, there are lots of sidecar taxis and several buses.

Terminal 2 of Cebu Airport is for international flights. The departure hall is shaped like a huge traditional Filipino long house, and it is pleasing to the eye (well, mine at least). Seven flights are advertised on the departure board; three are destined for Taipei in Taiwan, and none are going to destinations outside Asia.

We can make out several high-rise buildings in the middle distance, and I am not sure the highway network on the island can cope with the pressure of much more high-density development, which in my view is already at capacity, or to quote the jargon employed in British planning circles, it has reached 'severe' impact on the capacity of the system.

As the dawn breaks, it is clearly promising to be a beautiful day. There is a blue sky and white, fluffy clouds and there has been no rain since the small hours. Our Philippines Airlines 09:50 flight to

Tokyo takes off on time. From our window seats we can see scores of ships and then a large island, presumably Luzon, which occupies a location in the north of the Philippines archipelago. Soon, only white clouds can be seen below us.

After several hours in the air, we begin our descent into Narita Airport, situated some distance to the east of Tokyo. The first part of Japan I set eyes upon seems to be full of golf courses!

Our taxi driver who collects us from the airport is immaculately dressed in a suit and tie (this goes for just about every taxi driver we come across in Japan) and speaks a little English. He takes about an hour to reach our hotel from the airport, along a good dual carriageway which doesn't experience any congestion until we are about five minutes from our final destination in the centre of Tokyo. At one point, the road rises over a substantial bridge where we gain a sweeping view of Tokyo Harbour, complete with rows of shipping cranes. At the end of our journey, the driver even gives us his card.

Our hotel, the Royal Park Iconic Tokyo Shiodome Hotel, in my view lives up to its somewhat grandiose title. It is around 40 storeys high and our 27th storey room is quite spacious, as well as affording good views out over the city skyline. We are located centrally within the city within a distinctly upmarket district known as Shiodome, located just to the south of Tokyo Central Station.

After a couple of hours' rest, we discover a traditional Japanese restaurant within the hotel complex and we put ourselves through our paces – watery soup, uncooked fish, a spicy dip and several tiny but spicy courses. We opt for one meal between the two of us, which turns out to quite adequate.

We are dog tired by ten o'clock and decide this is the right time to go to bed.

Wednesday 1 March

The Hama Rikyu Garden

There's a great view down from the hotel's 24th storey breakfast area over central Tokyo and in particular as far as a railway nerd like me is concerned, onto the tracks leading to Tokyo Central Station. The icing on the cake is a gleaming white, sleek looking Shinkansen express train (more popularly known as a bullet train), comprising around 20 carriages long, covering the last few hundred metres before coming to a halt in the station.

After breakfast (egg benedict for Sylvia and an omelette for me), I enquire at the hotel reception about trains to Matsumoto for next Monday. The receptionist initially says we have to change trains at Nagano, but she digs around and eventually comes up with a direct 'limited express' train, taking just two and a half hours, which departs from the other main station in Tokyo, called Shinjuku Station.

After resting in the morning, we set out on foot/wheelchair in the early afternoon to visit the Hama Rikyu Garden. A young guy just outside our hotel asks if he can help us, as he sees me pushing Sylvia uphill. He is the first of what turns out to be quite a commonplace experience over the next couple of weeks - being approached by friendly and helpful Japanese passers-by who are keen to assist us when they see Sylvia being pushed in a wheelchair. It becomes one of our most endearing experiences of our time in Japan.

A few minutes later, we meet a guy whom I would put in his 70's called Amadi. He not only offers to help us with directions to the garden we wish to visit, but he also offers to come with us to the garden. I think this is called going the second mile. As soon as we reach the garden, the sun comes out, and the weather turns quite warm. We are told that there was snow here in Tokyo only last week. This is the perfect weather for walking, at least for someone from the temperate latitudes.

Hama Rikyu Garden - or Gardens as it appears in some publications – was reputedly owned by shoguns (leaders in Japan until the nineteenth century) when they were founded over three hundred years ago. The gardens are full of pink and white blossom and also include a field which is a luminous yellow carpet of what looks like rape seed. The gardens are popular and there are many people taking photographs, especially close-ups, of the blossom. Many of the photographers are elderly men, or elderly men accompanied by much younger women. And there are some powerful cameras on display.

Some way into the gardens, we encounter a hump-backed pedestrian bridge over a stream. I am struggling at this point to push the wheelchair over this bridge, whereupon a young couple rush up to us and offer to help push Sylvia to more level ground. We are almost being smothered in kindness on our first full day out in Tokyo.

In the evening, we partake of a very expensive sea bream in one of the hotel restaurants, which offers amazing views down on the still busy multiple railway tracks leading into Tokyo Central Station. The views also show a myriad of illuminated office blocks, which exude their own kind of mesmerising beauty. Downtown Tokyo has an amazing skyline, especially at night. Our meal and the atmosphere from this vantage point have induced a very relaxed feeling within us.

Thursday 2 March

A Loyal Dog, Meeting up with Tomoru, A Palace and a Tower

The different time zones we have passed through over the past couple of weeks seem to be catching up with us, and especially for Sylvia, who is asking for her medication at the earlier time than usual of 07:00 hrs this morning. (Usually, it is administered at eight.)

There's a new guy supervising entry to the breakfast bar in the hotel this morning, and he is insisting that everyone wears a mask. I call him the 'mask fuhrer'. I wave an official-looking piece of paper at him and say "Exempt" and carry on walking, unmasked, into the breakfast area. But this officiousness is counter-balanced by a very attentive waitress, so I don't have to collect anything from the buffet area.

This morning, we are off on a quest to visit an immortalised dog, or at least a dog statue, which is nearly 100 years old. The Hakika Dog Statue portrays a faithful dog, by the name of Atika, which used to wait every day at Shibuya Station for its owner to appear off a train at the end of each working day. The owner would then walk the dog home. However, the dog's owner, a university lecturer, died suddenly at work in 1936, and he therefore never came home again. But the faithful dog continued to wait outside the station for its owner to appear for a further nine years. It is Japan's best known faithful dog story. The story has been made into a film, starring Richard Gere.

Our taxi deposits us outside Shibuya Station, which forms part of an exciting New York 'Times Square' style creation at a meeting of several roads with neon signs beaming from buildings, and with lots of people milling around. The whole place is, unsurprisingly, very noisy. It's a great place to soak up the somewhat frenetic atmosphere, with the pedestrian footfall increased by the entrance to the station. This is definitely one of the liveliest parts of the city that we have experienced.

There is a queue of people waiting to have their photograph taken by the side of the famous dog statue, and I wheel Sylvia into position for her photo-opportunity. We also spend several minutes observing this busy scene. Eventually, we move on, and I push her for about 50 metres to a taxi rank. The driver who picks us up says that Shibuya has been at the centre of a major rejuvenation project for eight years, with a lot of disruption, but it all seems to be coming together now. It appears to me to be a place with a lot of energy.

On the way back to our hotel, our taxi travels on a main road directly underneath an elevated highway. Apparently, the viaduct is carrying the main highway to Osaka, so the driver tells us.

We take a quick lunch (organic curry) in a café close to our hotel and then we return to our hotel and prepare for the arrival of our long-lost friend, Tomoru, last seen by us in 2001, when he stayed at our home for a few months in the UK as a student at South Devon College, sent to us by the Japanese Ministry of Education.

Tomoru walks into our hotel reception at three o'clock in the afternoon, having travelled down from his home in Iwaki by train, about four hours away to the north of Tokyo. Almost as soon as we meet up, he is raring to go, and to be fair to him, he is also happy – he even volunteers - to push Sylvia in her wheelchair. He is keen to show us as much of Tokyo as possible in the limited time we have available with him. We have booked him into our hotel for the night. Tomorrow, the three of us plan to travel to a beautiful rural area about 100 miles to the north of this city where the three of us are also going to stay the night in a local hotel.

We soon leave our hotel on foot/wheelchair and navigate two short sections of subway before emerging near to the grounds of the Imperial Palace. We cross the outer moat on a narrow bridge and enter the palace grounds via a fortified gate. The palatial building itself is off-limits to the public, but it can be seen in the middle distance, where it seems to look out mysteriously in its ethereal grandeur at the real world from the far side of a small lake.

High rise office blocks form a fixed, unbroken line across the main road which separates them from the imperial gardens. However, Tomoru tells us that, despite the centrality of the Imperial Palace in Tokyo, no engineering operations, including tunnelling, are permitted beneath the imperial gardens. Maybe this is not too different from the situation in and under Buckingham Palace in London, but the contrast between the bustle of modern Tokyo and the seemingly withdrawn, secretive palace and its extensive gardens, seems stark in my opinion.

By four o'clock it is becoming overcast and the temperature has dropped, and a passing Japanese visitor to the gardens remarks to us that it is 'samui' ('cold' in Japanese) and she is right! Mercifully, there is no rain as yet, but it seems to be on its way. Tomoru's pace, however, doesn't slacken, although I manage to stop for a few moments to take some photographs of modern office developments which have been designed with attractive water features. We also catch sight of the classical entrance to Tokyo Central Station, which is impressive and takes me by surprise.

It's not long before we are heading down into another subway station, this time for a ride of half a dozen stops until we alight at the Tokyo Sky Tree, which at around 635 metres in height, is the tallest building in Japan, although certainly not (in my opinion) the most beautiful. Parts of the structure are spread out as antennae, which is perhaps the reason why it is called Sky Tree.

We ascend to a viewing platform near the top of the tower, just as dusk is falling. Among the magnificent views of the city, several features stand out. These include the key business district, some significant waterways and a myriad of bridges, and further out, the Bay of Tokyo and its many ships. Some of the railways can also be made out.

Before leaving the tower, we opt for a Chinese meal in one of the many restaurants within the Sky Tree development, complete with refreshing, hot China tea. I surprise myself at how much I enjoy the tea, as I am not a great tea drinker. It's now nearly seven o'clock and we have been on the go since three in the afternoon, and I have a couple of stiff limbs. Sylvia has also been stuck in her wheelchair for far too long, and she is beginning to feel the effects.

In the restaurant, Tomoru gives us a present. It's called Okiagari Koboshi, and it comprises two plastic characters who always bounce back if you knock them over. Tomoru says it portrays a Buddhist theme linked to resilience. They are also called 'roly-polies'.

Coming out of the Sky Tree Centre, we ditch the public transport option and hail a taxi back to our hotel, and finish up for the night ordering coffee in the hotel bar/dining room.

It's our first real chance of the day to find out what Tomoru has been doing over these 22 years since we last met. He tells us that he is still a teacher, and is about to change schools, which most teachers apparently have to do in Japan every six years or so. But he is still teaching English to junior high school students (13-15 year olds) and says he loves it.

Apparently, Tomoru has only just found out about the change in schools for him, and we are the privileged first to know; he hasn't even informed his wife yet. Tomoru explains that there is a lot of pressure for teachers to get promoted to managerial roles. However, he says that he still loves the actual activity of teaching in a classroom setting where he can relate to the students and he doesn't want to have a purely administrative role, which, he explains, is completely removed from involvement in the classroom in Japan. When we ask him what English literature he prefers teaching, he quickly says Shakespeare; absolutely no doubt about this. The allure of the bard is apparently not diminished in these parts.

As we go to our separate rooms for the night, I discover that I have mislaid my room key, so I trot back to reception and apologise for my transgression. The lady on reception, by the name of Tomkin, is remarkably cheerful about it, saying that she receives requests for replacement keys at least three times per day, so not to worry.

I then ask Tomkin about keeping some of our stuff in our room tomorrow night when we will be away from the hotel, taking a trip to the mountains some way to the north of the city, around a place called Nikko. She consults her manager and they offer me a reduced rate for the room for tomorrow night. However, after a lot more discussion and some consultations between the two of them in Japanese with me trying to guess the body language, they agree to waive the fee and we shake hands on it. And so to bed.

Friday 3 March

Discovering the Wild Country of Nikko

Our programme today is to visit the spectacular wild scenery in the Nikko National Park, where the three of us (Tomoru, Sylvia and I) will spend the night in a hotel, before returning to Tokyo tomorrow.

Our breakfast in the hotel is delayed by a long queue, with the surge of guests linked to the Tokyo Marathon. This means that we now have about 15 minutes to take some coffee and a croissant before the three of us leave the hotel, travelling light with just our backpacks. We catch a subway train and then walk a couple of hundred metres, still in central Tokyo, to Asakusa Station, which is a terminus on the privately operated Tobu Line. The station stands out architecturally and it seems to me to be akin to an Art Deco creation, with splendid proportions. We are fighting against the clock, and I am walking as fast as I am able with my stick, to try and keep up with Tomoru powering away pushing Sylvia's wheelchair.

We just about manage to board the Limited Express, as it is known, to Nikko before its departure time of ten o'clock, cutting it fine with two minutes to spare, and we wouldn't have made it apart from Tomoru's drive and determination. Our compartment on the train is comfortable; we have our own table, and the journey is pleasant and, especially for a foreigner, interesting.

Our train leaves on time and presses northwards through Tokyo's inner urban areas. Most of the dwellings in the central parts of Tokyo that we travel through are packed in closely to each other (as in many cities of course), but they are often interacting with their neighbours at different angles, and from what I can tell, usually with no recognisable garden or back yard and not much sign of any curtilage boundaries. The variety of angles and alignments of the eaves result in magical roofscapes and patterns of urban design; this is definitely not an unattractive urban landscape. After a while, we cross the Shumida River and travel through Tokyo's outer suburbs.

An hour after leaving Asakusa Station in Tokyo, the high housing densities begin to fall off, and urban gaps often accommodating rice fields start to appear; they are mainly yellow and dry-looking at first, but later on we also spot green fields. The scenery assumes an undulating character with distant, snow covered mountains on the horizon.

Our train terminates at the small town of Nikko at noon. This is the local centre for touring this wild and scenic area. Tomoru picks up a hire car he has previously booked from a dealership just off the town's central square; it is a small Toyota which is comfortable and has plenty of room for Sylvia and her wheelchair.

Tomoru is keen to make progress, and we journey into the Nikko National Park, which strikes me as a cross between the Lake District and Derbyshire, back in the UK. Tomoru, our driver in the hire car, negotiates a long series of hairpin bends through forested, mountainous terrain, where the air is clear and the area is almost devoid of people. Tomoru says he thinks we are about 100 miles from Tokyo and it feels like it. He is a more than willing pusher for Sylvia in her wheelchair, leaving me to try and catch up with them on my stick after we dismount from the car.

Our first stop is at a cable car run, but our initial excitement is a little deflated when we realise that they are only testing it, and it is not yet open to the public. However, the place is almost deserted, with clear air and beautiful views to be had of snow-clad mountains, and it is eerily peaceful and our spirits are lifted.

After a short drive, we park by a body of water in the mountains, known as Lake Chuzeni, which is sparkling in the bright sunlight. It seems like Japan's answer to Lake Ullswater, back in the UK Lake District. The sun may be out, but it is still quite cold, but relatively free of the summer crowds. Eventually, we find a café-cum-store open in what appears to be a lakeside resort, largely asleep in winter mode. We order a local, home-made curry, which we are ready for, after our somewhat depleted breakfast this morning, all those hours ago!

While we are eating our delicious curries, I ask Tomoru what his wife's reaction was to his forthcoming change of schools. He tells me that he didn't get around to telling her this news last night on the phone. For some reason, we all find this very funny and the three of us spontaneously burst out laughing. So, outside the school, we are still the only ones in the entire universe who are in the know about Tomoru's latest career prospects. Sylvia buys some fridge magnets in the store, predictably with scenes of Japan, to give out as presents.

A short distance from the lake, we visit the Kegou Falls, which are quite noisy as a result of the winter rain. We view this spectacular feature from across a chasm, which must be a factor in concentrating the noise in this constricted area. The waterfall crashes down over several hundred feet, gouging out a rock pool and generating a lot of spray and piles of deposited loose rock.

The design of the viewpoint enables Sylvia to get a great view of these falls in complete safety. I read somewhere that the Kegou Falls are considered by many to be the most spectacular falls in Japan. This is a sublimely beautiful and peaceful place, with views of mountains and valleys in several directions, where you can lose yourself in natural beauty. It's great just to spend time in silence, and drink it all in. Again, we are almost on our own enjoying this beautiful place.

Tomoru says he comes here fairly often, and it's not difficult to see why. This is one of several highlights of our time in Japan.

We drive to our hotel that we have booked for the night and check in at around five o'clock. The Fairfield Hotel where we are staying is isolated from its neighbours in its own extensive grounds, situated in open countryside, a good drive from the town of Nikko and its facilities. It is a beautiful place, with stunning scenic views in several directions. The main building has expensive looking finishes and gives the impression of being a spa treatment centre, which would not look out of place in Scandinavia or Switzerland. However, I am surprised to be informed that the hotel does not serve either breakfasts or evening meals. It advertises a caring environment, but the care doesn't extend to feeding you.

Tomoru, helpful as ever, says he will book a restaurant for us in Nikko for seven o'clock this evening, so we have nearly a couple of hours to put our feet up and relax, which is precisely what we need to do right now.

Just under two hours later, Tomoru drives us to a traditional Japanese restaurant in Nikko. The town is deathly quiet at this hour in the early evening; we are clearly a long way from the bustle and bright lights of Tokyo. The atmosphere in the restaurant, however, is warm and the staff are attentive and friendly. We order tofu, with a main course of chicken or trout. We are experiencing a perfect atmosphere, and then, whilst we are eating in the subdued ambience of the dining area, a road maintenance gang starts up a road works, complete with noisy drilling, just outside the restaurant.

"Do you know why they are doing this?" Tomoru asks.

"Is it because it is the end of the financial year?" I reply.

"Yes!" says Tomoru. "It's the same in every country!"

We find a convenience store on our way home and buy a few items for tomorrow's breakfast. Back in our hotel, and shortly after getting ready for bed, I take a look out of the bedroom window. The garden is illuminated, and after a while I observe that there are two foxes rummaging through the flower beds!

Saturday 4 March

Trainspotting in Japan: Locomotive C11 123 and the Edo Wonder Train

Sylvia has experienced a bad night. She can't climb into the bed, which is too high for her. We had to call for help at eleven o'clock at night and again at half past three in the morning, and the poor lady has spent a lot of time in the bathroom.

Tomoru, Sylvia and I eat our purchased breakfasts in our bedroom, after which I spend some time outside in the hotel grounds, taking photographs of the mountainous views. After helping us have a great time over the weekend, Tomoru says that tomorrow, instead of resting and chilling out, he will be taking a group of volunteers from his school to do community work, including beach cleaning, in his home town of Fukushima. The guy certainly has a lot of energy, as well as being community spirited.

Our first visit this morning is to a group of Shinto shrines in a woodland setting. The shrines, and several artefacts associated with them, date back to the seventeenth century. There is, however, little information about them in English. One of the structures, looking like a temple, refers to ritual cleansing and the importance of purification, with a date of 1603, but that's as far as the explanation goes in English. Unfortunately, my camera battery runs out at this point, and I discover that my back-up battery is flat as well. So, I have to revert to taking pictures on my mobile phone, which I find a bit of a pain.

We wander round the Nikko Toshogu Shinto Shrine, which seems to me to be the focal point of the group of religious buildings in this place. During our hour or so wandering around these beautiful structures, the place noticeably gets busier and louder and more congested. According to Tomoru, more and more people are arriving from Tokyo all the time. As we head away from the shrine, we notice that every parking space has been taken, and there is even a queue at the car park entrance, so it is as well that we came when we did.

Tomoru drives the car back to the hire car agency, whereupon the staff kindly drive us to the nearby Shimo Imaichi Station, where we watch a steam locomotive, number C11 123, sporting the name board 'Edo Wonder Train', shunting three carriages into a station platform, then decoupling from them and trundling onto a turntable. The black locomotive is a large, 2-6-4 tank engine (train spotters will know that this spells 'big'), which is accompanied by a freestanding tender, a most odd, almost unique arrangement. Tomoru thinks the locomotive must be at least 70 years old, but it looks in good condition and clearly receives a lot of TLC.

Once on the turntable, locomotive C11 123 hisses loudly as it releases steam, sounds its horn a few times and belches smoke all over the place, not that anybody seems to mind. The locomotive seems to be relishing being the centre of attention. It certainly is letting everyone know that it has arrived! And 'everyone' includes a myriad of faces lining the outer perimeter of the turntable, all concentrating on the locomotive. Not a few of the onlookers are female; some are the wives, partners, mothers, sisters or girlfriends of the men and boys present, and there are lots of small children taking in the scene. I had no idea that so many Japanese loved steam engines! There are cameras everywhere.

The disability access staff are helpful and efficient, as we are finding everywhere in Japan. We are taken onto one of the carriages waiting to be united with their steam locomotive, for a short ride through a green valley, hemmed in by mountains. But this is a ride with a difference. Several mainly young people, dressed up as Ninjas, are strutting their stuff up and down our carriage, whilst other Ninja characters are shouting at us from outside the train, some engaged in sword fights and generally causing merriment and mayhem. The playacting carries on until the steam train ends its journey in another small town with a busy station which is generally wedged in by mountains. At this station, we transfer to our Limited Express which will take us back to Tokyo. Even on a Saturday, or maybe because it is a Saturday, the line seems busy.

When we arrive back in Tokyo at the terminus station at Asakusa, there is a unanimous decision to opt for a taxi to take us back to our hotel. During our taxi ride, it's clear that Tomoru and our taxi driver are getting on like a house on fire. Tomoru says later that they discussed several matters. The taxi driver had asked how it was that Tomoru and ourselves knew each other. Tomoru said he explained to him that he had stayed with us in the UK 22 years ago. The taxi driver also said he had a wife in a wheelchair, and they shared a lot about accessible public transport. Another topic of conversation focused on sat navs. We have noticed how brilliant Tomoru is at just going up to people and chatting with complete strangers, engaging them in conversation in a very natural way.

We return to our hotel and arrange to meet up with Tomoru in half an hour's time. He disappears off to do some shopping for his wife, or so he says. Our friendly receptionist, Tomkin, then says "hello" and gives us a fluffy Easter Bunny! Shortly afterwards, Tomoru returns from his shopping expedition with a bag of oranges and bananas for us, which is a really nice gesture.

The three of us meet up for a final meal in our hotel bar, and we all opt for the chef's recommended pasta. Tomoru tells us he has just sent some photographs and a message to Junko, our Japanese friend in the UK, assuring her that all is well with us. Then, at a quarter past seven, he says his final goodbyes, picks up his bags and departs for Shinjuku Station (reportedly the busiest in the world) to catch his evening train back to Iwaki. We have had three amazing days with Tomoru, getting to know him once again and seeing places we certainly never would have seen, if left to our own devices. A few of the hotel staff have commented to us on our unusual and interesting friendship with Tomoru, and I get the impression that this is a rarity. We look forward to seeing him and his family in the UK before too long.

We receive a final 'selfie' photograph of Tomoru on my mobile phone. It's a great picture, showing him on a platform at Shinjuku Station, with his Shinkansen express train to Iwaki pulling into the station behind him.

Sunday 5 March

The Fellowship of St Alban's

Sylvia and I enjoy a very relaxed breakfast, especially as the numbers eating in the breakfast area in our hotel are significantly down on a couple of days ago, post Tokyo Marathon. And our breakfast is served graciously by our very keen-to-please waitress, Oyashiki (she wrote her name on a serviette, or I would never have got it right); she is lovely and nothing is too much trouble for her, probably on account of Sylvia's wheelchair and my stick.

At around ten o'clock, we amble down to the hotel's main entrance, where a waiting taxi takes us to St Alban's Anglican Church, located a stone's throw from the famous Tokyo Tower, which incidentally is no longer the tallest structure in the city, but in my view an altogether more elegant creation than the taller Sky Tree Tower, and Tokyo's answer to the Eiffel Tower in Paris.

St Alban's church sits neatly in the street scene, exhibiting an almost domestic scale and a pitched roof. It proves a bit of a challenge for wheelchair access, but we are met at the church doors and greeted by a couple of helpful worshippers who make sure Sylvia gains safe and secure access to the building.

The minister of St Albans, who is referred to as Father Michael, delivers a short sermon based on the character of Abram in the Old Testament. Father Michael expresses concern about the reference in the Bible passage in the Book of Genesis, where it refers to people whom Abram has 'acquired'; slavery was common at this time, although of course it is still not entirely eradicated today. The minister expresses the thought that these 'acquired' people could have been converts, as God's plan was for everyone to enter into a relationship with him. He concludes by saying that we should take as many people with us as we can by sharing the gospel with them, but not, of course, through enslaving them!

The church service is quite formal by our 'free church' standards or tradition, but early on in the proceedings we are offered the microphone and invited to introduce ourselves. We keep our comments short, and I am even applauded for my efforts!

We experience a genuine welcome at the end of the service, and we all shake hands with Father Michael en route to the adjacent coffee bar. The congregation is touching 100, and it mainly comprises expatriates, but not just Brits; there are Antipodeans, Americans and South Africans. There are several Nigerians and a few Indians as well as a handful of Japanese. Several come up to welcome and talk to us. A South African lady by the name of Aileen offers to help with pushing Sylvia to the coffee room at the end of the service. She and her husband Wilhelm are both air pilots. They also have strong links with Kenya, which keeps the conversation flowing; I never thought I would be saying anything in Ki Swahili during our time in Japan!

A Malawian guy named Sam, with strong links into student networking, also chats to us for some time and arranges a taxi for us after we say our goodbyes to all these friendly people.

The church also has a ministry among refugees and displaced people, which surprises me, as I hadn't been aware that this issue existed in a significant way in Japan. Apparently the issue is quite serious in some of the big cities like Tokyo.

In the afternoon, we wander through the subterranean arcades within easy walking/pushing distance of our hotel. We come across an American themed restaurant and order chicken and pancakes in maple syrup. A woman at the next table immediately offers her help in transferring Sylvia from her wheelchair to a seat at the table. She introduces herself as Yae, and says she is an artist and a musician. She tells us she enjoys the cultural scene in Manchester in the UK, when I let her know that this is my home town. When she tells us she aims to visit the city in the summer, I pass on our email address and other contact details in case she wishes to contact us whilst she is in the UK.

The rest of the day is dominated by packing all our stuff that we are taking with us for the next week or so into just one of our big cases (and our back packs), and packing the other big case to leave at our hotel, for collection on 15 March when we briefly return here prior to our flight the next day to London. We also consume a pizza in the hotel bar in the evening, and settle down for an early night.

Mike Fox

Biwa-ko Lake, near Kyoto

Hama Rikyu Garden, Tokyo

A Walk on the Wild Side

Shibuya, Tokyo

Sylvia and statue of the Loyal Dog, Shibuya, Tokyo

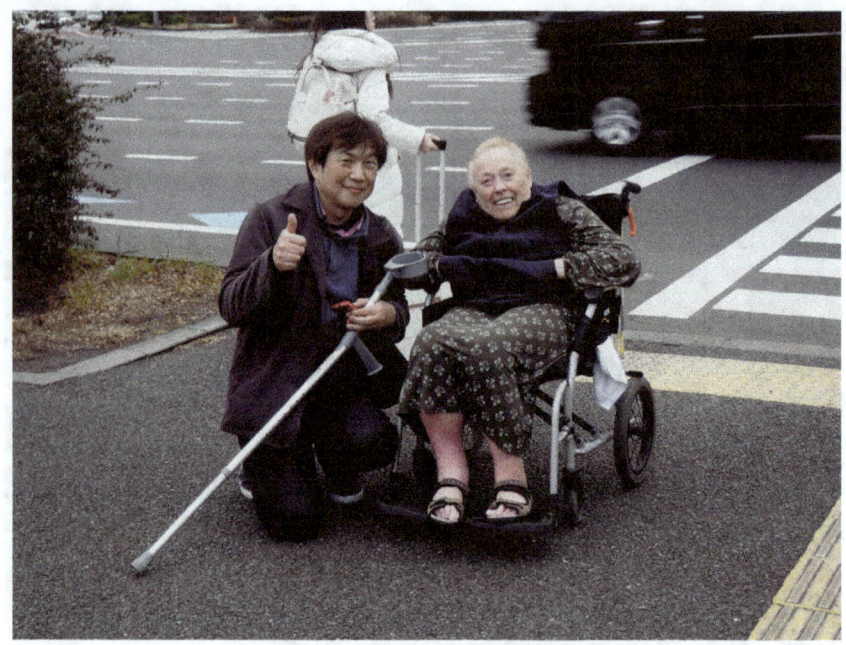

Tomoru and Sylvia, central Tokyo

Imperial Palace, Tokyo

A Walk on the Wild Side

Skytree Tower, Tokyo

View from Tokyo Skytree

Artistic display, Skytree

Rice fields en route to Nikko

A Walk on the Wild Side

Mountains en route to Nikko

Nikko Station

Lake Chuzeni, Nikko

Treescape, Nikko National Park

Mountains, Nikko National Park

Fairfield Hotel garden, Nikko

Kegou Falls, Nikko

A Walk on the Wild Side

Nikko Toshogu Shinto Shrine

Entrance to shrine

Shimo Imarichi Station and locomotive C11 123

Mike, Tomoru and Sylvia, Royal Park Hotel, Tokyo

Tokyo Tower, Tokyo's answer to the Eiffel Tower

Monday 6 March

The Limited Express to Matsumoto

We catch a taxi at eleven-thirty to Tokyo's vast Shinjuku Station in order to board the 13:00 hrs Choo Line Limited Express to Matsumoto, which is famous for its castle and is situated in the Central Highlands of Honshu.

Our taxi driver warns us that it will be touch and go whether we make it to the station on time to catch our train, and there is certainly heavy congestion in the city streets today. Firstly, he suggests taking a toll road, and then changes his mind, further adding to my stress levels, after I had thought we had left sufficient time to make it to the station without too much difficulty.

We are dropped off at Shinjuku Station with half an hour to spare before our train is due to depart. We are initially overwhelmed by the lack of any directions that we can make out within Shinjuku Station (including to the trains), and get the overall impression that we are entering a shopping hub rather than a railway station – and a crowded shopping centre at that. It seems strange not seeing anything pointing us to the trains.

Just as I am wondering what on earth to do next, a woman comes up and asks if she can help us, and makes enquiries as to where I need to show my JR rail pass. She accompanies us into a lift, and then puts us in touch with the railway access people, via the booking office to get our tickets for the journey. Without her help, I am convinced we would have missed our train; she is one of several ministering angels we encounter whilst we are in Japan.

A member of the access staff takes us, via another lift, onto our platform, and we board our train at 12:55 hrs, which is just five minutes before its departure time. I experience massive relief once we are seated in our carriage, and the express departs at five minutes past one. I am not sure if we are the reason for the five minutes delay in our train departing; Japanese trains are not known for experiencing delays.

After about 40 minutes into our journey, travelling initially in a southerly direction, the urban character of Greater Tokyo gives way to hilly countryside. I notice quite a lot of land instability and reinforced earthworks. A substantial amount of the forest cover looks disfigured with discoloured leaves, as if affected by pollution. My guess is that there has possibly been mining or industrial activity (or maybe earthquakes) at some time in the past to cause the disturbance in the landscape. Most houses in the towns we pass through are individually designed and are generally pleasing to the eye. Many buildings have complex pitched roofs, which add to their charm.

Our train passes through several tunnels as the terrain becomes more challenging. Some of the mountain peaks have a smattering of snow, reflecting the bright sunlight. The landscape assumes an Alpine feel, peppered with several chalet-style homes, loosely scattered over the slopes.

A drinks and 'chocky' biscuits lady with her trolley comes along, and this is a godsend, as we haven't eaten anything since our breakfast, which seems like a long time ago.

The train passes through an inter-montane valley, weaving its way through thousands (if not more) silver birch trees, their trunks glistening in the bright sunlight. The sky takes on a pristine blue.

At Matsumoto Station, which is also the final destination of our train, we are met by the access people, who help us off the carriage and onto the platform. They then help us book our tickets to

Kanazawa, which will be our next port of call on Wednesday. Finally, and amazingly in my view, one of the railway staff offers to walk with us to our hotel, bringing our large case with him.

Fortunately, our hotel is only a short walk along a couple of streets from the station, but it probably would have necessitated a taxi ride but for the railway employee's kindness.

We check into our hotel, the Hotel Tabino, which is basic, bordering on Spartan, but we feel it should be adequate for our two nights here. It is certainly clean and tidy.

The hotel receptionists advise us on where we can find a traditional Japanese restaurant, and after an hour's rest we follow their directions, walking/wheeling past a couple of blocks, and arriving at a small door facing an even smaller lift. We squeeze (just about with the wheelchair) into the miniscule lift and exit it at level 4, where we make progress along a narrow corridor. Just as we encounter two concrete steps, out of thin air, as it were, four people appear and carry Sylvia in her wheelchair over the steps and into a room, which I can only describe as Old Japan – it has dim lighting, a low ceiling, wood panelling and a domestic scale of uncomplicated furniture, and I feel that I am being transported back several centuries.

My Japanese phrase book works overtime as we order off the Japanese menu. We enjoy fish soup, followed by slender strips of beef set in rice, and then China tea, and scoops of ice cream. Our dining experience is superb and the friendly waitress needs no persuasion to take a couple of photographs of us with my camera.

On arriving back in our hotel lobby, our peace is shattered by a couple of Americans criticising our hotel, easily loud enough for the entire reception area to hear. I am not impressed.

We have an early night, and I succeed in finishing my Le Carré novel.

Tuesday 7 March

Matsumoto Castle

We are blessed with another glorious morning and we look up to a clear, blue sky. Our hotel has an airy and spacious breakfast area, which is concealed from the main entrance and comes as a bit of a surprise to me, and there is plenty of choice in what to eat and drink.

The main reason to decide to include Matsumoto in our Japanese itinerary is its famous castle, which is officially designated as a national treasure, and that is where we make for today. We hire a taxi to take us for the journey of approximately one mile from our hotel to the castle entrance, through the centre of the town.

Matsumoto Castle dates from the sixteenth century when Japan lay in the grip of several warring factions. Its original sole purpose was for strategic warfare. The castle comprises three towers. The central tower, which is the highest, contains five levels, each with an ornate and beautiful roof. It sits in extensive, landscaped grounds, which are contained by a series of moats, which add to the attraction and beauty of the grounds. The English version of the public information notes says that the castle was used by Samurai warriors, primarily for watching the moon and drinking sake! This sounds like they had got their work/life balance sorted out satisfactorily!

In the background we can see a line of Alpine shaped mountains, several with snow-clad peaks, beneath the clear blue sky. The air is cool, but pleasantly so. We take a break and sit and watch the castle over our bottles of coke.

Access within the castle is only possible by very steep wooden steps, which resemble ladders or rungs, and which rules out wheelchair access completely. When I ask if there is a lift, this is met with "Don't you realise this is a national treasure?" This means that Sylvia has to sit out this experience of castle exploration and await my return from exploring the interior of the castle. Fortunately, it is sunny and there is a gentle breeze.

I have to explore the interior of the castle without my shoes which I am required to surrender to the security people at the entrance. Even my stick is wiped clean. Inside the castle, there are lots of uncluttered passages to enable the samurai to race around, defending the place. The wooden floors and dividing partitions are glistening as a result of their constant polishing, creating a surreal, other-worldly effect.

Facing a second set of steps as steep as ladders to get up to the next level, I decide to call it a day on my exploration of the castle and make my way across the castle to a series of downwards steps or rungs. The only way back down to the ground floor is to sit on each stair and descend, one bump at a time, and I do it very slowly indeed, with full concentration on not crashing down and breaking a limb. I am observed doing this by some worried officials with deep, furrowed brows, and I am half expecting that I am going to slip and do myself some real damage. I am quite relieved to make it back to ground level in one piece.

We have the time, and hopefully the energy (and the OK in principle from the Tourist Office that the route is suitable for wheelchairs), so I push Sylvia out onto the roadside and circumnavigate the castle grounds. This enables us to see the castle from various angles. It is such a photogenic place and clearly one of the great sights of Japan. The peripheral highway also passes Matsumoto City Hall and includes views of a Catholic church, something of a rarity in Japan, and a Shinto shrine (known apparently as the Matsumoto Shrine), which is somewhat less of a rarity in these parts.

Looking at a map of the city, I can see a succession of temples and shrines forming a clear line to the east of the city centre. I count a dozen or so such religious structures, along a north-south axis. No one I come across is able to give me an explanation, but the focused alignment of so many of these structures seems to point to something more than just chance. There is also a close juxtaposition of Buddhist temples and Shinto shrines.

Back in the town centre, we beat a path back to our hotel. On our journey, we eat lunch in a café with a veranda, and we find ourselves almost sitting in the street, which adds to the atmosphere. We enjoy ice cool apple juice and scone-like savoury creations with cream cheese, and with a broccoli infill for Sylvia and a keema curry infill for me. What is also attractive is that you can see the food being prepared, and it's as though you have entered someone's private kitchen.

We also come across a rarity so far in Japan – the sight of post cards for sale – which prompts us to buy some with perfect pictures of the castle. We follow what looks like one of the city's main thoroughfares, crossing the Metoba River where someone on a sandbank appears to be photographing wildlife, and eventually we make it back to our hotel.

At around five o'clock, Sylvia and I go down to the hotel's 'happy hour', where we are joined by a Japanese teacher of English who tells us that she lives in the city. She says she is very keen to meet up with us for a meal tomorrow, but I don't think this is going to work. Her name is something like Keiko, but a little more long-winded.

In the evening, we discover a Korean restaurant, just around the corner from our hotel. As has already been our experience, several diners charge out of their seats and help carry Sylvia's wheelchair over the threshold and into the restaurant; it's almost as though they have been waiting for the opportunity.

The lady who is running the place appears not to know a word of English, but we are able to point to various pictures and she's all smiles anyway, so that we are able to order our meals successfully. Inside the restaurant, everyone is speaking quite loudly, but it's all good natured. Although the food is good, the lady restauranteur can only make cold tea, and absolutely no coffee. This means that I have survived the entire day on two cups of coffee!

Wednesday 8 March

The Trek to Kanazawa

I somehow manage to pack our big case in 30 minutes. I write a few post cards and then go and post them at a nearby convenience store. At midday, we order a taxi to take us the short journey to the railway station. Even Matsumoto Station, serving a relatively small city, has a track layout bordering on the complex, and the upper level of the station provides a great viewing platform to observe all the railway traffic comings and goings, which is a must for nerds like me. I could happily spend a couple of hours up here, watching all the train movements.

We need to change trains to get to Kanazawa, our next destination. At 15:05 hours, our Limited Express leaves Matsumoto on time and takes us on the first leg of our journey as far as the city of Nagano. The train follows the side of a substantial valley with mountains beyond, although the view over this landscape is punctuated by several long tunnels. Sylvia is in the middle of asking me a question, but by the time we have passed through the fifth tunnel I've forgotten it. The train driver seems to enjoy sounding the horn as we approach level crossings. It is turning into quite a warm day, and the rice fields appear to be very dry.

At the industrial city of Nagana, we change trains. We are taken to a large waiting room by the access staff. It strikes me as ironic or even funny that everyone in the room is immaculately well behaved, despite the fact that a samurai film of extreme violence is showing on a large screen.

Our train to Kanazawa is a Shinkansen, the archetypal bullet train. I can't resist taking a couple of photographs of the sleek train as it draws into the platform. These trains are huge and long, but they also display a chic beauty. Even with the assistance of the access staff, Sylvia manages a spectacular fall as she is being manoeuvred into her seat on the train. And it takes several people to ensure she is safely settled.

Another plus for the Shinkansen, in addition to its high speeds and comfortable seats, is its superb toilets. In fact, from our observations, many Japanese loos are amazing, and I think they are probably the world leaders in this important aspect of our daily lives. Many toilets have heated seats and covers which rise electronically as soon as they sense your presence, and include a number of water features to ensure you get a really good wash, including an integral bidet. There are even diagrams to explain which parts of your anatomy are going to be affected by which jet of water, some of which border on the pornographic. The toilets on our Shinkansen are positively palatial, with plenty of room, in sharp contrast to most toilets on aircraft!

Looking out of the train window to our left, there is an impressive wall of snowy and icy, rocky mountains, looking scary but magnificent. I try to do the scene justice with my camera, which is challenging from this high speed train. The mountains provide a stark contrast to the endless parallel levels defining the rice fields on the flat valley floor.

Some of the settlements along the railway are quite industrialised, but the visual impacts of these manufacturing centres are contained by the topography, and the prevailing sense is of an attractive landscape.

Our Shinkansen draws into Kanazawa where it terminates. It appears that the larger stations served by the Shinkansen have a special section (and platforms) reserved for use by these trains (sometimes on different levels to the rest of the railway network). It seems to be a sign of prestige for a town or city to 'graduate' to being put on the Shinkansen map.

It is a struggle hauling our large case in addition to two rucksacks and pushing the wheelchair. (We would have had real problems if we had brought both our large cases on this leg of our travels.) A major challenge to us is the tactile surfaces in railway stations to assist blind people. I need to book our ongoing tickets to Hiroshima for our next journey on Friday, and this takes half an hour, during which one of the railway access staff looks after Sylvia. Then Sylvia needs to find a disabled persons' loo. We are approached several times by people offering to push our large case.

At one point, a young lad, probably still in his teens, approaches us and asks if he can help in any way. At this moment, I realise that I have left my stick in the disabled toilet, and I make my way back to retrieve it as fast I am able to make progress unaided. When I return to where Sylvia is, the young lad is still with her, crouched down, chatting to Sylvia at her level, when he could have easily left her and gone on his way. He asks us where we are trying to get to before he leaves us. This to me sums up the prevailing attitude of spontaneous helpfulness and kindness that we are experiencing all over Japan.

Eventually we make it to the taxi rank. As pleasant as our taxi driver is, he lands us at the wrong hotel, and we are really dog tired by now. We have to order a second taxi to get us to the right hotel, which fortunately doesn't take long.

We find a street level restaurant next to our 'correct' hotel and revive a little after marine-flavoured pasta. We are back in our bedroom before ten o'clock and crash out pretty quickly.

Thursday 9 March

The Gardens of Kanazawa

From our hotel bedroom window, we get a view over tiled roof tops to a railway viaduct, with trains crossing it every 20 minutes or so. We chill out after a lazy breakfast and generally recuperate.

We order a taxi for midday to take us to two gardens which have high reputations in Japan (which itself, of course, has a worldwide reputation for beautiful and interesting gardens). Firstly, we are taken to the Kewoku Gardens, which go back to 1546, not long after Magellan landed in Cebu (and interestingly, the Portuguese also became very interested in Japan around this time).

The quality and landscaped settings of some of the buildings and several wide, tree-lined boulevards that we are driven along give me the impression that Kanazawa is a prosperous community; it is certainly a green one. However, among the hi-tech structures, we go past some traditional looking wooden buildings which appear somewhat dilapidated, and yet possess an attractive character, worthy of conservation. We also pass by what seem like two pairs of Geishas, dressed in almost impossibly tight clothing. (Tomoru said to us the other day that Geishas are dressed so tightly that many of them experience problems with going to the toilet! I think he was being serious.)

At the entrance to Kewoku Gardens, I ask the receptionist about the admission charge. The lady at the desk looks at me and says: "You are very old, senior, so it is free to you". I think she is trying to be helpful, and I guess on balance that I am encouraged by this remark! (Or at perhaps my bank balance is.)

Kewoku Gardens are evidently popular, and quite crowded; maybe this is not the ideal place for quiet meditation! But the gardens are attractive, and they are enhanced by several beautiful lakes and ponds in addition to their special landscaping features. The main problem for us is the rough gravel surface of the paths, which maybe are more in keeping with the ambience of the gardens than concrete paths, but they make wheelchair pushing a challenge, although there are no really steep gradients. We progress into the gardens as far as a delightfully designed wooden chalet which accommodates tea gardens; it all looks so serene and peaceful. Unfortunately, we have no time to stop and take some tea.

Our taxi driver is waiting for us as we leave Kewoku Gardens. He takes us to the smaller Guokusen-en Gardens, a short distance away, also in the city. We have to tackle quite a steep gradient, but on a firmer path than those in the earlier, Kewoku Gardens, and the wheelchair (and Sylvia in it) eventually make it to the summit.

These gardens are much smaller than the earlier ones we saw, totalling around one hectare in extent, and they lie in a hollow, focusing on a small lake or large pond. It is said to have been designed by a Korean landscape gardener (Kim Yeochol) in the early seventeenth century, and they are arranged in the form of the Chinese character for water (mizu). Their location in a bowl enables you, from a higher position, to look at the whole creation in one glance. The gardens comprise a series of islets in the lake, together with bridges, and even a stepped, artificial waterfall, which is all the more amazing, considering it is around 400 years old.

An elderly couple in a building overlooking the gardens approach us and ask us where we are from. They then ask if they can have their photograph taken with us, and of course we oblige; we are very happy to. They are just a couple of the many friendly faces we have encountered during our time in Japan. They also give us a present of two origami birds with flapping tails!

We rest up for a couple of hours in our hotel in the late afternoon before catching a taxi around five o'clock, which takes us to a seafood restaurant suggested by one of our hotel receptionists. The driver takes us on an interesting journey towards the coast, much of it in parallel with a single track railway line, which weaves its way narrowly between houses and workshops, depots and factories, crossing the road we are on via a level crossing. The railway seems to be active and in good health, which is confirmed a few minutes later as a two-car diesel multiple unit rattles past us.

The recommended seafood restaurant that the taxi delivers us to lives up to its billing. We are ushered into a private booth and personally attended to by a young lady called Maina (I think that is her name). After a fairly long discussion, we negotiate our way off sashimi, which I realise is raw fish, which was the way the discussion initially was headed. We opt for a fish by the name of 'buddi', which is strong tasting and served with white Japanese radish and rice.

Maina tries really hard to communicate in English as much as possible, putting my attempts to use Japanese in phrases to shame. She even agrees to pose for a photograph with Sylvia, without wearing her face mask. Even though our meal is a surprise for our western taste buds, we thoroughly enjoy it and feel completely relaxed with the décor and attentive staff. It's been a really great gastronomic experience for Sylvia and me.

Our taxi ride back to our hotel passes the cruise liner terminal (showing that Kanazawa really has arrived in the international world of tourism) and also a line of illuminated cranes by the dockside. But, in the dark, I don't manage to get a glimpse of the sea itself.

We are back home just before nine o'clock for a relatively early night.

Friday 10 March

Taking the Shinkansen to Hiroshima and meeting up with Fujio and his family

The continuous spell of clear, sunny weather has come to an end and this morning is overcast. We check out of the Daiwa Roynet Hotel, and bid goodbye to the friendly reception staff. A short taxi ride later lands us at the city's main railway station.

We take the Thunderbird Ltd train bound for Osaka, but discover that the width of the carriage aisle is too narrow to enable Sylvia in her wheelchair to pass to her allocated seat! A couple of American tourists come to our aid and offer up their seats by the carriage doors. This is a kind gesture; otherwise, we would have been stranded between carriages for the journey to Osaka.

Our train passes a gigantic statue of Buddha overlooking the rice fields. Its sheer size is amazing which is somehow amplified by its open countryside setting.

As in other parts of Japan, there seems to be a detailed interplay between rice fields and urban development, creating something akin to a piano keyboard effect. Again as before, hardly any dwellings appear to have curtilages, as far as I can make out. A huge lake (Biwa-Ko) appears to our left, before we stop at Kyoto. The water in this lake looks dark blue at first, but this changes to a paler blue later on. Our first views of the lake are in a pristine landscape setting, but it becomes more urbanised the nearer we get to Kyoto.

We change trains in Osaka, where we manage to grab a sandwich to stave off our hunger. It is clear from looking out from the train that Osaka is a huge city, with many high-rise buildings. One difference between Japanese cityscapes and their European equivalents is the traditional Christian heritage. In Europe and America, such religious based structures often tend to break up the overwhelming commercial and secular feel of cities, even if they are not always used for worship.

In Osaka, we transfer to a Shinkansen (bullet train), a gleaming white monster of a train with the title of Sakura Super Express, which will take us to Hiroshima. The Shinkansens are the flagships of the Japanese railway system. Our train leaves on time, and Hiroshima is the fifth stop where we will disembark. Moreover, the carriages are more spacious than in our previous train, and Sylvia can gain access to her seat quite easily. I also find myself sinking into the comfortable spaciousness of mine. I wonder how the British next generation of high speed trains – known as HS2 – will compare with the Shinkansen, that is, if we ever succeed in having HS2 in Britain.

It's now a gloriously sunny afternoon. Our train gives a real sensation of speed and it is exhilarating. A lot of the journey is spent passing through tunnels, and I wonder whether this is newly constructed track.

Our bullet train arrives in Hiroshima station in the early evening, close on five o'clock. We are directed to our destination by our taxi driver. Unfortunately, it turns out not to be our hotel, but the bell captain of this hotel, as she is referred to, takes it upon herself to take our heavy case and wheel it round the corner to our correct hotel, with me pushing Sylvia in her wheelchair in hot pursuit of our luggage.

There's not a lot of time to rest in our new hotel, however, as Fujio, one of our students who stayed with us in the UK, is due to meet us here at seven o'clock, together with his daughter, Saori; they are taking us out for a meal this evening. He arrives bang on seven and drives us to his chosen restaurant. Just outside the restaurant, we meet his wife, Yoko, and we are all invited into a private room which has been prepared for us. Again, the meal is basically seafood – and lots of it.

As we start talking over our meal, interesting details emerge from Fujio from his stay with us in the UK over 20 years ago; he remembers the names of the two dogs that we had when he lived with us (Megan and Dino), and then he shows us photographs he took of himself in our home, of Sylvia, and also of the two aforementioned dogs.

Initially, Yoko says she is busy tomorrow and therefore would not be able to join us for the day. However, later in the evening as our interactions become more relaxed, she says that she would like to join us. I offer to take the train tomorrow to Yamaguchi, where they live, but Fujio says he will drive over and collect us, and suggests a ten o'clock pick-up time at our hotel.

Saori has a Japanese-English translation tablet, which she puts to good use in our conversations over the dinner table. Although Yoko and Saori make out they don't speak any English, they surprise me and possibly themselves by how many English words they do know and how well they communicate with us. Saori tells me she is about to graduate from Junior High to Senior High School. She also gives us a letter which she has written to welcome us to Japan, which is a sweet gesture and really appreciated by us.

Our unfamiliarity with Japanese seafood causes some amusement on their part as they watch us attempt to eat and then react to a variety of 'surprise' delicacies, such as octopus, squid and seaweed. On the whole, Sylvia and I enjoy the food placed before us, and it has been a good experience, both culinary and educational.

At one point, they mention the name of a restaurant they wish to take us to tomorrow evening, which is called Sanzoku (meaning 'bandit' in Japanese), and I respond with the phrase 'sounds good', which they consider sounds almost the same. They find this unintentional pun of mine very amusing, and it acts as a kind of ice breaker moment. It certainly causes a lot of laughter.

Fujio and his family drop us off outside our hotel at ten o'clock. We then say goodbye to Saori and express the hope that we will meet her again, maybe in the UK.

Unfortunately, later in the evening, Sylvia comes out in blotches and itches from something she has eaten, but it calms down during the night, maybe after an hour or so and she says that there is no lasting discomfort.

Saturday 11 March

The Peace Museum and an Unusual Bridge

It's a race against time to be ready to meet up with Fujio and Yoko in the hotel reception at ten o'clock this morning. Sylvia puts in a tremendous amount of effort, but we still fall short by ten minutes in the end. Fujio and Yoko are of course already waiting for us, and they drive us from our hotel to the famous Hiroshima Peace Museum. This is somewhere I felt I needed to visit during our time in Japan.

I can sum up my experience of visiting the Hiroshima Peace Museum in one word – chilling. The main part of the museum experience is walking through a dark passage, which twists and turns past a series of illuminated exhibits set into the walls, and with the aid of an audio device which explains each of the photographs and other items on display in more detail. There is no shortage of information in this museum. Visitors are asked to be quiet or at least restrict any conversation to a minimum, and this request is largely observed. The ensuing silence adds to the museum's impact, heightening my awareness of the enormity of the terror which unfolded onto the residents of Hiroshima when the atomic bomb fell on their city.

We are introduced to scores of graphic descriptions on the impact of the horrors of war when the world's first atomic bomb was dropped on the city of Hiroshima on 6 August 1945, resulting in over 140,000 deaths and many more mutilations and other injuries. The items on display contain touching descriptions of so many individual tragedies, in many cases to people just going about their daily domestic lives, travelling or at work. I learn that

Hiroshima was considered by the Allies during World War Two as one of four potential targets in Japan for nuclear bombing; in the end, only two of them were actually selected, the other being Nagasaki, further to the west on the neighbouring island of Kyushu.

It seems that the primary reason Hiroshima was prioritised for bombing was the rapid build-up of military ordnance factories in the city over the preceding months and that the overall reason for the use of these atomic weapons was to bring about an early end to the Second World War.

Early on in the exhibition, I come across a black and white photograph of a streetcar, taken the day before the bomb was dropped. The poignant image stays with me (and has done since I returned home), as the 'quiet before the storm'. There is also an aerial photograph of Hiroshima, displayed in tabular form in a separate room. It shows the city as it was immediately before the bomb struck; then it shows a blinding flash, followed by a scene of total devastation. It is a truly terrifying set of images. There is no glamorisation of war in this museum.

At some point walking through the darkness, I become detached from the others, and I manage to end up being the first to arrive at the museum reception area. I sit down and wait for everyone else to appear. As I am sitting there in the reception, I am approached by a guy who says he wants to chat to me, because he noticed me pushing Sylvia in her wheelchair yesterday, just after we had alighted from the taxi outside the station and went to the wrong hotel; he says that his wife had remarked that we seemed like an amazing couple! He tells me his name is Horst, and that he was born in Germany in August 1945, a few days from the bombing of Hiroshima, but he is now a Canadian citizen and lives in Toronto.

We spend around half an hour in conversation, mainly about the pointlessness of war. We both agree that it would be a good idea to invite the North Korean generals to visit this museum and see for themselves the horror of war, and that it is no game. We also discuss the need for the armaments industries to find markets to enable them to test their products, let alone the complete waste of money nuclear weapons cost. We exchange email addresses. I think there is a good chance that we will keep in touch.

I am eventually reunited with the rest of our party, and we leave the museum. We wander along the banks of the Motoyasu - Gawa River, which is one of the distributaries of the Hiroshima River Delta, and find a spacious, airy café where we chill out for a few minutes over a few snacks and drinks. Inside the cafe there is a piano, in a glass case, which is almost intact and which apparently, quite remarkably, survived the bombing of the city.

An original domed building, reduced to a ruined core, and now known as the A-Dome, has been preserved in the extensively landscaped Memorial Gardens which form a tranquil backdrop to the Peace Museum. This building, until the bomb fell, was in use as an industrial promotion hall. Also within the park, we reflect briefly at the cenotaph for the A-bomb victims; through the concrete inverted U of the structure, we can see, in an almost direct line, the Peace Flame and beyond that, the A-Dome.

Back in Fujio's car, we leave the city of Hiroshima on an urban highway, which runs inside a curved barrier, resembling, to my mind at least, a giant vegetable cloche. Fujio drives us through attractive countryside to the valley of the Kintai-kyo River, as far as a remarkable bridge, known, perhaps unsurprisingly, as the Kintai-kyo Bridge. The bridge over the river was constructed in 1673 and it comprises a superstructure of five timber arches built on stone foundations. The river is flowing rapidly over rocks and stones below the bridge, and several people, mainly children, are splashing around and playing in the water.

Sylvia is wheeled up to and pushed across the first arch of the bridge, which is fairly gentle and step-free so as not to impede the wheelchair. However, this is as far as Sylvia can make it, as the subsequent arches are significantly steeper. Fujio and I manage to clamber across all the arches and make it to the opposite bank of the river. In addition to the beautiful landscape, there are interesting traditional wooden buildings lining the roads on both sides of the river, which hopefully are protected for posterity; I can't possibly imagine that this is not the case, as they contribute significantly to the historic scene.

As we walk across the bridge, with its spectacular views up and down the valley, Fujio says that it is likely that he will be moved to a new school within the next year and that he has no say in the matter. He enjoys the school where he works as head now, but national policy is to rotate everyone every five or six years; just as we have learnt in relation to Tomoru.

We also talk about the development of the city of Hiroshima. Fujio says its population now exceeds one million, and we agree that the rejuvenation of the city in recent years has been a success story. The city certainly gives off an air of affluence and wellbeing, and the treatment of the area around the Peace Museum with its attractive park and riverside, has been very successful, both environmentally and socially.

A couple of black guys are sitting on the river bank, talking to some Japanese girls. Fujio says we are near an American military base, which explains the presence of quite a few young black guys in this area, as we have seen almost no black people anywhere else in Japan.

Around dusk, we stop at a colourful restaurant in a wooded gorge. Its name is Sanzoku, which means 'bandit', which is what set us off laughing in the restaurant last night in Hiroshima. There are several fires burning in braziers and there are drums sounding, with the lilt of a traditional Japanese guitar (koto) strumming in the background. This all generates an atmosphere of mystery as the light begins to fall around half past five o'clock. A small stream next to the restaurant is filled with large, colourful carp.

Fujio's wife, Yoko, sets off to see how quickly we can be served. In fact, one of my lasting memories of Yoko is of her running to find out something or discover a shop or a parking place or some other information; she is always on the go, often at speed and she seems to be super fit. I wonder whether she keeps a record of the number of paces she makes each day!

Some of the artefacts, furnishings and trappings inside the restaurant conjure up an image of Old Japan, and we soak up the ambience. The cuisine is excellent, and again it is traditional Japanese, with an emphasis on seafood.

Back at our hotel, Fujio says he will collect us tomorrow at the later time of eleven o'clock, but at this point we have to say goodbye to Yoko, who is not able to join us tomorrow. We invite both of them and Saori over to the UK to stay with us next year.

Sunday 12 March

The Torii Gate at Miyajima

True to his word, Fujio collects us from our hotel at eleven o'clock to take us to an island called Miyajima. He warns us that at weekends, the traffic will be heavier than usual. Unsurprisingly, therefore, we get stuck in a traffic jam, and after we have been stationary for 15 minutes, our Sat Nav calls out: "Be patient!" So there we have it - wait your turn! There is also a railway running parallel and close to our road, so being stationary has its compensations for a railway nerd like me.

The shortage of parking spaces at our destination is also an issue. Fujio's patience and perseverance, however, finally pay off, and he succeeds in finding a parking space behind a closed-off area, and before long, the three of us, plus wheelchair, are safely aboard a ferry carrying us on the short trip from the mainland to the island of Miyajima.

It looks like the world and his dog has taken the opportunity this Sunday to visit the island that we have just disembarked onto from the ferry. However, most of the island is dense mountainous woodland and 99% of the visitors seem to be limited to exploring a section of the island's northern strip. But what a strip! In addition to temples and shrines, one particular shrine, known as Itsakushima Shinto Shrine, has caught the attention of the world, and in December 1996 it was designated as a World Heritage Site.

Perhaps the most impressive part of the religious complex is the Torii Gate, which stands fully in the water at high tide. It comprises a slightly curved roof, supported by two sturdy pillars, and some smaller supports lower down. It certainly resembles a gate. The wooden structure, painted in bright vermillion red, is nearly 17 metres tall and is located about 200 metres off shore. It contrasts with the deep blue of the sea and the dark green vegetation backdrop of the island, which rises to over 500 metres. It is one of the truly iconic sights of Japan.

A couple of women, maybe in their 20s, come up to us and ask Fujio if we would like our photograph taken with the Torii Gate in the background. Fujio assures me that they approached him with the offer, not the other way round! We feel that we are among friends.

The Torii Gate guards the Itsakushima Shinto Shrine, which is also painted red. The shrine comprises several interlinked halls and passageways, all on stilts, and which sit on water at high tide. There is a statue which Fujio says is of the Buddha, but I haven't yet got my head around how Buddhism and Shintoism relate to each other. But it's clear that Buddhist temples and Shinto shrines are often located in very close proximity to each other. Fujio does give me the impression that much of Shintoism is connected to ancestor worship.

Fujio, however, does make the observation that there are many gods in Japan, but interestingly goes on to cite commerce and studying as two of them!

Some of the natural inhabitants of Miyajima Island are small deer, and they are mixing freely with humans, mainly, I suspect, in the hunt for food. I spot several of them eating leaflets, which I wouldn't have thought were edible taking the concept of inwardly digesting written material a tad too far. A deer comes up to me, as if to say: "hello friend, how about a meal?", and nudges me with its nose. But I have no food on my person and it soon wanders off in search of pastures new.

Just as we are moving back to the ferry departure point on the island in the late afternoon, a Japanese family starts talking to Fujio, and they are asking him where we are from. They then welcome us to Japan, which is a nice gesture.

There are several contemporary buildings and structures on the island, some constructed in steel as well as timber. But it seems to me that they have achieved a high measure of architectural harmony and they don't detract from the beauty of the island.

The weather is starting to change as we travel in the ferry back to the mainland. The temperature is also dropping markedly. Fujio then drives us back to Hiroshima. On the way, we see extensive views out over the narrow sea to a series of mountainous islands to our right. This really is a beautiful part of the world.

We go for one last meal before Fujio has to drive back to his home in Yamaguchi. We enjoy a Chinese meal in an upmarket hotel which adjoins the railway station. Over the meal, we do our best to persuade Fujio to come and bring his family over to stay with us in the UK next year. It would be great if we could pull it off, and he is certainly not ruling it out. He even accompanies us to the ticket office in the station, where we book our tickets for our journey tomorrow to Kyoto.

It's final goodbyes at the hotel. Fujio says he couldn't believe that we were serious about our visiting Japan at first. Mind you, we weren't that sure about how serious we were in the beginning of our deliberations, either! I still blame our son Nathan for planting the seed in my head after we arranged to come over to celebrate his wedding in the Philippines.

Monday 13 March

Travelling to Kyoto

Today is history in Japan. It is the day face masks are no longer officially required in public places. Fujio had said yesterday that he thought many Japanese would continue to wear them, and so far he has been proved right. This morning, I would say that at least 75% of the population are still voluntarily wearing facemasks.

I have mislaid my mobile phone charger. The hotel receptionists point me in the direction of an electrical store – they tell me: "Just walk through the station at level 2, and you can't miss it". While we are passing this way, we check on disability access arrangements for the train to Kyoto which we will be catching later in the day, and which will involve changing trains at Kobe.

On the south side of the station, we see one of the termini for trams in the city. This includes the starting point for the tram to Miyajimaguchi, where we boarded the ferry yesterday.

As per instructions, we find the electrical shop quite easily, and we purchase a new phone charger. I must make sure I don't lose this one! We then opt for a quick early lunch in the station shopping centre. We are both suffering from our 'systems' not working properly; Sylvia's system is not appearing to work at all, and mine is suffering from the opposite effect. We collect our baggage from the hotel and slowly move them a couple of hundred metres to the station.

Just as we enter the main entrance concourse of the station, two chatty schoolgirls, maybe in their mid-teens, come up to us and ask if they can help us with our baggage. They ask us where we are from (as so many Japanese do) and when I ask them what they are planning to do today, they say they are coming to the station to visit one of the cafes. Although this station has everything and has already been recently extended at a higher level to accommodate Shinkansen trains, major work is now in progress to achieve a further extension and improvements. Japanese railways don't appear to sleep on their laurels!

On the first leg of our journey to Kyoto, our sleek Shinkansen train glides out of Hiroshima on the most elevated level of tracks. We look down over extensive rail freight yards, attended to by colossal blue electric locomotives (the same colour as the freight locomotives in China). In most places, when viewed from the train, the intensively developed urban landscape is broken only by rice fields, many of them patchy and seemingly ripe for infill development in this highly urbanised country. It looks like every flat parcel of land is either under urban development or is used for rice cultivation. It seems as if about half the journey to Kobe, where we change trains, is in tunnels.

Changing trains at Kobe is simple enough, and we even don't have to change platforms. As usual, we are looked after well by the disability access staff, who take the stress out of the operation.

Just after the train for Kyoto leaves Kobe, we can see a line of cranes in the distance and a few ships out to sea, reminding us that Kobe is a major port as well as being one of the world's great ship building cities.

Our train arrives at Kyoto on time. Kyoto Station is huge and possesses a cavernous central hall that would stand comparison with New York's Grand Central Station. In a city with so much history and with such a strong emphasis on conservation, the construction of such a gigantic and tall (16 storeys) station building, unsurprisingly, was highly controversial, and there were strong public protests. In its defence, I would say that the new station certainly celebrates rail travel and being so spacious, it definitely enhances the experience for travellers using it. This, in my view, has to be an important factor in the overall equation.

Although I don't have an intimate knowledge of the geography of Kyoto, it seems to me from my brief stay in the city, that most of the traditional areas which need to be protected from unsympathetic development are located at some distance from the main station. The neighbourhoods that I observe surrounding the station, including the environs of our hotel, are fairly unprepossessing modern developments that look the same or at least similar the world over. However, I accept that I could have missed some important details in the vicinity of the station, but from what I observe over a couple of days, is that the impact of the new station on the historic character of this wonderful city is minimal.

The One Thousand Kyoto Hotel is plush and attractive. Our bedroom is easily twice the size of our previous accommodation in Hiroshima. And we enjoy good (if a little on the expensive side) meals in one of the hotel restaurants.

At the reception, the staff inform us that they have received a message from a lady by the name of Kyoko, asking them to inform the hotel and ask for a favour on my behalf. Initially, in my slightly exhausted state, I can't work out how reception knew that I had a problem with my mobile phone charger. But it demonstrates that Kyoko knows exactly where we are. It looks like we are on course for a good day in Kyoto tomorrow.

Tuesday 14 March

Meeting Kyoko in Kyoto

The small hours bring new problems. Sylvia falls from her bed onto the floor on two occasions. In between these crises, I notice from my newsfeed that a rail strike is going to happen in the UK on 16 March, the day we return home. I immediately get on the phone to our travel agent, Mike Coles, who advises me that all our railway company (Great Western Railway) is required to do in a strike is to grant us compensation for our unused tickets and maybe pay for a Thursday night stay in a hotel near Paddington station, and that this could be the appropriate way forward for us.

I then ring our friend Angela with the latest news regarding our homecoming. She says she will discuss with her husband Mike whether he could collect us from London Heathrow Airport, but they will need confirmation that he can take the leave from work to do this. A couple of phone calls later, we learn that Mike is both able and willing to do this. This kind offer takes quite a weight off our minds.

Kyoko, whom we are meeting up with today, is a former student who stayed with us in our home in the UK whilst she learnt English, a couple of decades ago. She refers to us as her British parents, which is a huge compliment for us. We have kept in touch with each other over the years (especially at Christmas) and we are really looking forward to meeting her again after such a long period.

We meet up with Kyoko in our hotel reception, where she is already waiting for us – inevitably, there are hugs all round. She is instantly recognisable after two decades. (She doesn't say whether we are also!)

Kyoko tells us that she has booked a taxi driver for the day to show us some of the sights of the city. The taxi driver is an avuncular guy by the name of Kato, and he collects us from the hotel entrance right on time. He greets us and explains his proposed route with the aid of a large street map of the city, which he unfolds in his cab. His English is fluent (based on a few years living in California) and it soon becomes clear that he has an excellent knowledge of Kyoto, and he sets out by way of introduction with a few key facts about the city. An interesting feature of his map is that public no-smoking areas are clearly highlighted in yellow, and these include a couple of neighbourhoods and several streets. What a great idea, I think.

We learn from Kato that Kyoto has a population of around 1.5 million, placing it in the top ten most populous cities in Japan. It became capital of Japan in the eighth century AD, but in 1867, the ruling shogun handed over their power to the Emperor, who moved the capital to Tokyo. The city is located in a valley, apparently with limited scope for easy expansion, and it couldn't keep up with the growth of Tokyo, which is now the centre of a super conurbation, even by world standards.

Kato is keen to share his love of Shintoism with us. When I ask him to explain the difference between Shintoism and Buddhism, Kato says that Shintoism is about happiness, peace, health and prosperity, whilst Buddhism deals with suffering. He says that whereas Buddhism has a founder (the Buddha), Shintoism grew in a spontaneous, organic way, here in Japan, and that there are no sacred texts as such, unlike in Buddhism. (I understand that Shintoism is also theistic – even multi-theistic, whereas Buddhism is not theistic, although Buddhists do not refer to themselves as atheists.) He also says that because the two religions deal with different aspects of life, it is possible to be an adherent of both religions without compromising your integrity. I thank him for his explanation, which is the clearest I have heard so far in our time in Japan.

Our first site on Kato's itinerary to visit on our travels in Kyoto is the Fushimi Inari Taisha Shrine, on a hillside on the southern edge of the city's urban area. It is a Shinto shrine dating from the ninth century, constructed in honour of the fox, so I guess it is an appropriately good place for the Fox family to visit! Apparently, the fox is seen by Shinto adherents as a messenger of the harvest god and is therefore popular with farmers.

At this shrine, there are many torii, or gateway structures (the guidebooks say ten thousand), which form a covered (and coloured – bright red) walkway, which we make our way through (Sylvia included in her wheelchair) up the side of a hill, as far as the main Shinto shrine. These torii, or pillars with a connecting lintel overhead, have been donated by people over many years, in search of, according to Kato, money and a good time.

Kato explains a few more things about Shintoism as we make it to the shrine, which is high up on the hill. He tells us that there is no recognised founder of the religion, and its roots are here in Japan. He says that the religion has around eight million gods. (Is this a record for a religion? I wonder.)

When we arrive at the shrine, Kato encourages us to give coins and make wishes. When I decline, Kato asks me why I am turning down the opportunity of seeking a good time and satisfying my needs. I tell him, that as a Christian, I can pray to God for anything at any time, so therefore I don't need to make offerings to Shintoism. Kato then says that I don't have to believe it, but I can still go through the motions. I tell him that I respect his religion, but it's a case of thanks but no thanks regarding the ritual. Fortunately, this incident doesn't seem to affect our enjoyment of each other's company, which is very evident in our conversation and body language.

It's a hot day, and we slake our thirst, courtesy of a vending machine within the shrine complex. Kato tells us that the concept of supporting the torii financially is very popular with the business community in Kyoto. The line of torii ascending the mountain looks sleek and elegant, although the gradient is quite a challenge to get Sylvia along the covered way in her wheelchair. I am slightly surprised, however, that they have not cashed in with a café on the site, in view of the immense footfall attracted to this interesting place.

I am also surprised at some of the new developments which are clearly within the setting of the shrine complex, and therefore affect its visual impact. The new architecture can only be described as Brutalist and completely out of keeping with its spiritual neighbour. Also, and perhaps not entirely in keeping with the spiritual ambience, a group of Geishas in extremely close-fitting clothing can be seen walking through the complex.

Kato then drives us to a Buddhist temple called Sanjusangen-do. It dates from the twelfth century AD and it was built by the emperor. It adjoins a beautiful garden, with cherry blossom already flowering, which seems to be ahead of almost everywhere else in Japan, judging by what we have already seen. The garden is themed 'Hope for the Future'. This is a sentiment that is difficult to take issue with.

Inside the main 120-metre long hall of the temple, there is statue of a goddess called Kannon, Goddess of Mercy. She is definitely a 'wow' factor and she is surrounded by a thousand of her disciples, all armed and in dark gold and made of steel or some other metal. Unfortunately, we are not allowed to photograph them, which is a shame because they are incredibly photogenic. There is also a huge statue of the Buddha, dating from 1274, accompanied by the sight and aroma of incense smoke.

Kato tells us that at the front of this Kannon parade, there is a line of deities, for example of medicine, the sea and thunder, and one which intrigues me – protector of Buddhist teaching (the Assura). The two religions are certainly closely intertwined.

There is also an annual archery festival (every January), started in 1606, originally featuring samurai firing arrows the length of the hall, which is impressive by any standards. The records also show that the successful target rate is very high.

After leaving the temple, Kato drives us into one of the historic areas of the city, in a neighbourhood known as Gion, where there is a network of narrow lanes. He stops his taxi in one of the main streets, called Hamani-koji, and asks if I want to alight and walk along the street, saying he will stop a few hundred metres further along. I grab this opportunity with both hands and walk alone along the street, taking my time and admiring the traditional architecture of the street scene.

The buildings aligning the street display a delicate cadence with varying roof heights, several timber facades (with even more wooden houses along some of the narrow alleyways splintering off from Hamani-koji), and quite a few first floor balconies. Different coloured lamps, looking like illuminated globes, dominated by red but also in orange, yellow and white, adorn many entrances and add to the ambience of the street. There are lots of pedestrians and relatively few, and entirely slow moving vehicles in this delightful area, where the maximum building height seems to be limited to three storeys.

Within this atmospheric area, I feel that perhaps the only visual issue is the dense amount of overhead wires and cables, which appear incredibly intricate and complicated and distracting from the traditional character of the street scene. Having said this, I quickly get used to them.

We come across a traditional noodle house, displaying wonderfully ornate calligraphy in a number of signs at its roadside entrance, presumably setting out what's on offer inside. We take off our shoes and enter the establishment, and walk through several intimate chambers until we reach the furthest, innermost small dining area, located next to a typical Japanese rock garden. It gives me the sensation of going into the bowels of the earth, as we walk further into the establishment, away from the noises of the street. Our traditional meal of noodles is exquisite and we relax for a while in this lovely place before re-joining Kato and his taxi.

There is time to visit one more important site in Kyoto – Nijo-jo Castle. It dates from the seventeenth century, when it was built by a popular shogun leader by the name of Tokugawa Iyeasu at a time when there were around 50 separate feudal shogun domains in Japan. The castle made Tokugawa Iyeasu a top dog in military terms, and shoguns from all over Japan would come to the castle to do business with him.

Inside the castle, we are requested to take off our shoes. Even just wearing our socks, the wooden floors creak in response to being walked over; we are told that the creaking effect was deliberate – to warn off intruders! There are 'primitive' paintings of tigers and cougars on the castle walls. The castle was also the place where an historic meeting took place in 1867 – this was when the shogun rulers gave up their power to the Emperor, who then moved the national seat of power from Kyoto to Tokyo. This also marks the start of democracy in Japan.

Although Kato is a veritable mine of information about the castle and Japanese history in general, I don't really get it as to why the shoguns decided, apparently off their own bat, to give up their huge powers to the emperor in 1867. The guidebooks don't really help, either. I mean, why would you voluntarily give up absolute power, and for what benefit? Did the shoguns know the writing was on the wall for them? But the transfer of power from the shoguns to the emperor did take place – this is an historic fact - and furthermore, it took place through an agreement, ratified from within this castle.

We leave Nijo-jo Castle to the sounds of Auld Lang Syne coming from somewhere within the body of the castle, and we are accompanied on our outward passage through the castle gates by a small group of school students and their teacher. From their body language, they appear to be a close-knit group, enjoying each other's company.

Kato drops us off outside our hotel; he has been a great driver and tour guide, as well as fun to be with. He welcomes us back to Kyoto for another tour visit, and who knows? I would love to meet up with him again, as he is so enjoyable to chat to – and Kyoto is one of only a few places I have ever visited where I have a strong desire to return, having, in one day, just scratched the surface of all this wonderful city has to offer.

It has also been a joy to have met up again with Kyoko, who has been an excellent companion throughout the day. She even brings a special message from her mother, thanking us for making the effort to contact her daughter again, but we really wouldn't have missed this opportunity for anything.

Kyoko, Sylvia and I enjoy a final traditional Japanese meal together in a classy restaurant near the station. Kyoko then walks back with us to our hotel before we hug each other for the last time and say our final farewells. Fortunately, there is a fast and frequent evening train service back to her home in Osaka, so we don't have to worry about her hanging around on a station platform for long at night. It's been so good to see our 'Japanese daughter' again after all these years and to know that she is in a settled relationship and that her family is fine. She says she will try and improve her English and come over to the UK and see us before too long. We will look forward to that.

Our friend from home, Angela, texts me to let us know that her husband Mike has got approval for a day off work and will collect us from Heathrow Airport on Thursday afternoon.

Wednesday 15 March

The Super Express to Tokyo

Our aim this morning is to visit the famed railway museum in Kyoto, which we have heard so much about. We check out of our hotel by 10:30 and order a taxi. However, our trip is ill-fated, as the museum is closed for the day! I try all the entrances and attempt to find anyone associated with the place, but alas, there are no signs of life, no one to talk to, just enticing views of several railway locomotives, tantalisingly close but inaccessible, through the glass panels of the museum. So near and yet so far!

A second problem now presents itself; we are out on the streets, in an area of the city that we don't know at all, and we haven't a clue which way to go in order to locate a taxi. Our initial idea was to book a taxi from inside the museum, which of course is no longer an option. We have a train to catch early in the afternoon, so there's no panic, well, not just yet. One guy in the street that I get talking to points me towards a town square, and at the opposite side of an extensive pedestrian area, we come to a main road.

I try to flag down a couple of passing taxis, which just continue to drive past us. I then chat to a guy whose English is quite good, and he thinks we may have quite a walk to find anywhere to attract a taxi – when all of a sudden, a taxi draws up, seemingly out of the blue, and the driver agrees to take us back to our hotel, which he does. This little adventure – or misadventure – could have had a very different outcome for us.

It's turning out to be another hot, clear day with wonderful blue skies. We decide to chill out back in our hotel over a couple of cold drinks. My glass is filled and refilled with cold, refreshing water by the friendly hotel staff. The Thousand Hotel in Kyoto has been a great experience for us, with a wide variety of breakfast options for us to take advantage of, and staff who bring your choices to your table.

We arrive at the Kyoto main railway station just after midday, and we are booked onto the Hikaki Shinkansa Super Express, which is a fast train to Tokyo, stopping at Nagoya, Yokohama and a couple of other stations. I am really impressed at the information on the electronic destination board on our platform, which shows no less than six trains are bound to depart for Tokyo within the next hour. And this isn't even the rush hour!

Once on board our train, I get chatting to a smiling rail hostess, mainly about the possibilities of being able to view Mount Fuji from the train. After a short while she hands me a sheet which informs us that the train is scheduled to pass Mount Fuji, which can be viewed on the left hand side (the side of the train where we are sitting) at 15:50 hours. Such precision! And such helpfulness from such attentive staff.

Our express train pulls out of Kyoto, and before long it is passing through woodland and open countryside. Some of the mountains have been extensively scarred by quarrying, producing artificial and near-vertical cliffs. We also pass through urbanised areas and cross several rivers which appear to be seriously short of water, although even the resplendent blue of their reduced flows, and in some cases trickles, reflect the clear sky and add beauty to the landscape.

A lady selling snacks off a trolley works her way along the carriage, and we buy coffee, water and chocolate almonds. The train slows down through an extensive urban area, past large rail yards, tower blocks, and possibly one cathedral (an unusual sight in Japan), before stopping at Nagoya station. This is clearly one of Japan's great cities, the fourth largest in the country according to my guide book. We pass a long freight train, hauled by an impressive giant blue electric locomotive.

Pulling out of Nagoya after a brief stop there, we pass a marina with several pleasure craft, before cutting through more affluent suburbs, with housing climbing the hillsides at what appear to be much lower densities than on the plain. (As in so many areas, residential areas seem to climb both physically and socially.) Then it's back to green rice fields, interspersed with urban developments, occupying an extensive flat plain with distant mountain peaks. Again, we are observing the national competition for land between urban development and rice cultivation, which seems to be being played out all over Japan.

Around an hour after departing from Kyoto, the landscape becomes more undulating, the mountains appear closer to the railway, and the rice fields seem to be holding their own, and we pass through a few tunnels. The rivers we cross have more water in them than hitherto. We pass a huge, modern looking Sony factory, then several lakes, waterways and a couple of marinas. Our train stops briefly at Hamamatsu, a not insubstantial settlement, although less of a 'concrete forest' than Nagoya, but again with its own suburban rail system. A lot of people board the train here. Most people are still wearing face masks, now two days after they are no longer required to do so.

I think we pass some tea fields. So far, we have not seen any sheep or cows anywhere in Japan. We pass through more tunnels, with multiple mountain ranges on our left. The train makes a brief stop at Shizudea after crossing a wide river. Again, this is a sizeable town with some high-rise developments. While we are in the station, we are overtaken by (presumably) another Tokyo-bound train.

At around ten minutes to four, the hostess apologetically advises us that the weather is too cloudy to get a view of Mount Fuji. However, shortly after her announcement, the train slows down and the sun shines through and burns away the clouds. As we come to a brief halt at Mishima, there it is on the skyline to our left – the snowclad peak of Mount Fuji with its steep, icy sides, glistening in the late afternoon sunlight, looking down almost overbearingly like a colossus on this small town. The mountain must be several miles away from us, but it is an immense, dominant feature in the landscape, looking quite magisterial. My photographs don't do the scene justice, but it is a huge 'wow' factor for Sylvia and me.

Shortly after leaving Mishima, in between the tunnels, we catch a few glimpses of the sea. Like in the UK, you are never that far from the sea anywhere in Japan.

I suggest eating in our hotel in Tokyo this evening, unless Sylvia is up for a long walk; she says OK, as long as I give her a piggy back. Sylvia is striking a very hard bargain here!

We slow down for the large port city of Yokohama, past Toshiba and NEC plants, and stop for a while. The urban mass of Yokohama seems to run seamlessly into greater Tokyo, and somewhere in this vast metropolis, we stop once more at Shinagawa.

Our train slows down to a crawl, travelling alongside local services as we enter central Tokyo. As we prepare to disembark from the train at Tokyo Central Station, our stewardess presents us with two small complimentary pictures, one of Mount Fuji and the other of the nose of a Shinkansen bullet train. We have had some great rides on trains in Japan, and our Japanese Railway passes have saved us a lot of money and time.

Back at the Royal Park Hotel, who should we see in the reception but Tomkin, who gave us our Easter bunny last week, and who also helped Sylvia when she had her fall in the small hours. She brings our suitcases to our rooms, and then says: "It would be nice if you could meet my son in England; he has no religion except me." There's a challenge for us, and we give her our email address.

Our flight back to London from Haneda Airport is scheduled to take off tomorrow morning at 09:50 hours, requiring us to check in at the rarefied time of 07:50 hours, and we set our alarms for 05:30 hours; this is depressing stuff.

We eat in a small Italian restaurant just opposite the hotel, opting for spaghetti bolognaise and tiramisu. We are feeling very tired by half past eight this evening.

We crash out for an early night.

Thursday 16 March

Sayonara Japan

The alarm on my mobile phone sounds at the ridiculous hour of five-thirty am. I check out of our hotel at reception and find a lone taxi waiting in the parking area right outside the hotel, just as Tomkin had said. I commandeer it and leave our baggage with the driver before going back inside the hotel and bringing Sylvia down to the taxi in her wheelchair.

Even at six-thirty in the morning, the traffic in central Tokyo is a tad above light and our driver takes a toll road to Haneda Airport. We are driven along at a brisk pace, skirting the port, with its serried ranks of cranes. It's already a glorious, sunny day; spring has certainly sprung in Japan.

Haneda Airport is much more centrally located in relation to the city of Tokyo than Narita (the airport we flew into, just over a couple of weeks ago). It is located virtually on the coast. Our driver drops us off at the Departures Hall at seven o' clock, in good time for our flight.

There is time for a quick breakfast at the airport before the disability access staff take us onto the plane. Our British Airways flight is non-stop to London Heathrow. Our Boeing 787 takes off a few minutes late and we have clear views over the city of Tokyo, the sea and even Mount Fuji in the distance – but the latter view doesn't have the impact that we had of the towering, icy volcano that gave us such a 'wow' factor as we viewed it from our train yesterday.

Our flight crosses the International Date Line, which is a first for me, not that I know much about it at the time. The woman who is occupying the seat next to mine tells me she is returning home from a work trip. She is an engineering consultant and she is involved in a rail project with Hitachi, the world-famous Japanese train manufacturers; her specific area of expertise is centred on maximising the use and efficiency of batteries. Quite a specialist area, me thinks. She has managed to fit in some travelling whilst she has been over here, including walking near Mount Fuji, so it hasn't been entirely work-centred. It's her second work based trip to Japan this year.

It's a long flight to London, which takes us over the Arctic, and it lasts nearly 15 hours. At some stage I doze off to the sounds of Kekele and Rumba Conga, but not into anything resembling deep sleep. I also tune into an interesting BBC documentary on the Irish band U2, and it focuses on a number of individuals whose lives have been affected by their song *I still haven't found what I'm looking for*. One guy in particular cites the song as the trigger for him deciding to say goodbye to his long term girlfriend in order to join the Jesuit priesthood! We don't get the girlfriend's reaction to his changed direction in life on the programme…

We fly over the green fields of England below thick clouds, before touching down on time at Terminal 5 at London's Heathrow Airport. It's been a long flight, but we have been well looked after by the excellent cabin crew; absolutely no complaints.

There is some disagreement/confusion between the aircraft crew and the Heathrow ground staff over Sylvia's onward passage in her wheelchair, resulting in an hour's delay before we can leave the vicinity of the plane and work our way through the airport terminal to the arrivals lounge. But all's well when we get there and we see our friend Mike, who has been patiently waiting a long time for us. He carefully and safely drives two very tired travellers back to the West Country, for which we are truly grateful.

Traditional Japanese restaurant, Matsumoto

Matsumoto Castle and mountains

Matsumoto Castle

Matsumoto Castle and Moat

A Walk on the Wild Side

Matsumoto Station

Mountains and river, en route to Kanazawa

Kewoku Gardens, Kanazawa

Tea Garden, Kewoku Gardens

A Walk on the Wild Side

Kewoku Gardens

Guokusen-en Gardens, Kanazawa

Slightly quirky contemporary architecture, en route to Hiroshima

Traditional contemporary architecture, en route to Hiroshima

Fujio, Yoko, Saori, Mike and Sylvia, in a restaurant in Hiroshima

Yoko and Fujio, Hiroshima

Tramcar in Hiroshima, taken the day before the dropping of the A-Bomb, Hiroshima in August 1945, Hiroshima Peace Museum

Total devastation after the A-Bomb, Hiroshima Peace Museum

The surviving A frame building, Hiroshima

Peace Park, Hiroshima, Showing the A-Dome and the Cenotaph for the victims of the A-Bomb

Colourful kiddies, Hiroshima

A-Dome and Motoyasu-Gawa River

Cenotaph and A-Dome, Yoko, Sylvia and Mike

Kintai-Kyo Bridge

Gang of Four (Fujio, Sylvia, Yoko and Mike), Kintai-Kyo Bridge

Sanzuko Restaurant

Old and new trams, Hiroshima

Fujio, Sylvia and Mike at Miyajima

Torii, Miyajima

Itsakushima Shinto Shrine, Miyajima

Itsakushima Shinto Shrine

Looking across to the mainland, Miyajima

Tram terminal, Hiroshima

Fushumi Inari Taisha Shinto Shrine, Kyoto

A Walk on the Wild Side

Torii at the shrine

Kyoko at the shrine

Roofscape at the shrine

Blossom in the grounds of Buddhist Temple of Sanjusangen-do

Mike, Sylvia and Kyoko in the temple grounds

Mike Fox

Streetscene in Gion in Old Kyoto

Entrance to our restaurant, Gion, Kyoto

Kyoto Castle

New entrance hall, Kyoto Station

A Walk on the Wild Side

Arrival of our bullet train to Tokyo, at Kyoto Station

Misty view of Mt Fuji

www.ingramcontent.com/pod-product-compliance
Lightning Source LLC
LaVergne TN
LVHW021959060526
838201LV00048B/1625